GETTING IT ACROSS

A Guide to Good Presentations

Carole M. Mablekos

Professional Publications, Inc. • Belmont, CA

How to Locate and Report Errata for This Book

At Professional Publications, we do our best to bring you error-free books. But when errors do occur, we want to make sure you can view corrections and report any potential errors you find, so the errors cause as little confusion as possible.

A current list of known errata and other updates for this book is available on the PPI website at **www.ppi2pass.com/errata**. We update the errata page as often as necessary, so check in regularly. You will also find instructions for submitting suspected errata. We are grateful to every reader who takes the time to help us improve the quality of our books by pointing out an error.

Getting It Across: A Guide to Good Presentations

Current printing of this edition: 1

Printing History

edition number	printing number	update
1	1	New book.

Printed in the United States of America

Professional Publications, Inc.
1250 Fifth Avenue, Belmont, CA 94002
(650) 593-9119
www.ppi2pass.com

Library of Congress Cataloging-in-Publication Data
Mablekos, Carole M., 1938–
   Getting it across : a guide to good presentations / Carole M. Mablekos.
      p. cm.
   Includes bibliographical references and index.
   ISBN-13: 978-1-59126-063-9
   ISBN-10: 1-59126-063-9
   1. Public speaking. 2. Visual communication--Technique. 3. Communication of technical information. I. Title.

PN4129.15.M33 2006
808.5'1--dc22
                                                        2006044796

Table of Contents

About the Author v

Preface vii

Acknowledgments xi

Introduction xiii

1   Preparing Your Oral Presentation 1

2   The Main Parts of Your Talk 13

3   Designing Effective Visual Support 21

4   Managing and Handling Visual Support 45

5   Delivering Your Report 55

6   Twenty Surefire Tips 67

Appendices 71

Further Reading 85

Index 89

About the Author

Carole Mablekos has been affiliated with Drexel University since the early 1980s, teaching public speaking, technical writing, organizational behavior, and business writing courses.

From 1994 to 1999, she served as project manager for P.R.I.D.E, an NSF-sponsored effort aimed at developing innovative ways to deliver education to working professionals who want to return to academia for additional training or new degrees. This project provided a significant impetus for Drexel's distance learning programs over the last decade. For this program, she has developed several web-based courses: Introduction to Entrepreneurship for Engineers, an undergraduate course; and Communications, a core course in the Engineering Management Graduate Program. This course has been running continuously on the web since 1999.

Previously, Dr. Mablekos served as the coordinator of the writing center at the Philadelphia College of Pharmacy and Science and of the technical and business writing program at Temple University. She has also taught at the University of Washington, the University of Pennsylvania, and Cabrini College. In addition to editorial consulting in engineering, medicine, and chemistry, she has conducted faculty development workshops for technical and business writing, seminars for professional publication, and on-site writing and public speaking courses for architecture and engineering professionals.

Other publications include a book on oral presentations for students and young engineers, *Presentations That Work*, IEEE Publishers, N.Y., 1991, and an audio-course for chemists and chemical engineers, *Technical Writing and Communication*, American Chemical Society, 1988. She has also coauthored numerous articles on distance learning.

Dr. Mablekos holds a bachelor of science degree in education from Alverno College, a master of arts degree in English from Virginia Polytechnic Institute, and a doctorate in English from Purdue University.

PROFESSIONAL PUBLICATIONS, INC.

Preface

For the things we have to learn before
we can do them, we learn by doing them.

—Aristotle

Just as you can improve your public speaking skills by doing as many presentations as you can, I had to learn to teach public speaking by actually teaching it.

The role of teacher of public speaking was thrust upon me suddenly by some very sad circumstances. Some years ago, right at the start of the term, a colleague died suddenly in a weekend sports accident, leaving five sections of public speaking uncovered. Our distraught department administrator assigned me to teach in his place.

Although I had taught some presentation techniques in various technical communications classes, I undertook this new task with much sadness, reluctance, and trepidation. But I soon discovered that public speaking was a wonderful thing to teach. It was a real joy to watch students improve so quickly, progressing in a single term from being fearful of taking the stage to standing proudly as confident and articulate presenters.

With the goal of helping you do the same, I've covered in this book the basic principles of speech communication. I've drawn these from years of observing presentations by scientists, architects, and engineers—students and professionals; from current research in presentation techniques; and even from the knowledge about public speaking that has accumulated over thousands of years. A common observation is that public speaking is probably as old a practice as speech itself. The Stone Age hunter may have won extra respect from his tribe by standing up in front of painting on a cave wall and delivering a good technical briefing about the latest antelope or mastodon hunt.

Nevertheless, many otherwise highly intelligent and talented people regard this most ancient of human activities, as a task to be greatly feared and carefully avoided if at all possible. If you are among that group, this book can help you make the transition from apprehension to mastery. If you already enjoy making presentations, this book can help you polish your skills.

One of my objectives in this book is to show you how to design your presentations for maximum effectiveness, whether in your class, career, or community. Good speech design derives from a proper focus: You must focus first on your real purpose and on your audience, then on your organization of content and mode of delivery. This book stresses the need to think critically about how much and what kind of content you have so that you can find the best organization for the information you want to present.

Another objective is to build your facility with the standard tools of oral presentation. Computer-supported presentations are the norm nowadays, and you need to know how to select the right tools and deploy them with ease and effectiveness and without getting tangled up in technological excess.

Of course, developing a really effective presentation technique takes vigorous thought, hard work, and plenty of practice, along with some attempt to raise one's talk above the ordinary. It's not enough to gather a great pile of information and simply dump it all on your audience. You need to select content and convey its meaning so that you really get it across and make it stick.

In *The Craft of Scientific Presentation*, Michael Alley points out that scientists and engineers need to respect their material and their audience enough to make some strong effort in terms of presentation style:

*Strong presentations require both content and style.
Content without style goes unnoticed, and style
without content has no meaning.*

I fully agree. Useful and important material deserves to be more than just covered. If you have something worth saying, a presentation that's so low-key as to be boring does as great a disservice to your ideas as a presentation that's merely flashy. To present your points forcefully, you will need to connect to your listeners' minds in the most effective way you can achieve. Style, neither a luxury nor a frill, thus plays an important role in conveying content and interpreting meaning.

Aim therefore beyond mere adequacy for your presentations. The combination of good content, good design, solid speaking style, and plenty of practice can lead to outstanding presentations, the kind that people will remember.

—Carole M. Mablekos

PROFESSIONAL PUBLICATIONS, INC.

Acknowledgments

I would especially like to acknowledge the students and professionals who contributed examples of their work so that this book could be firmly grounded in real-world presentations. Most of what I have learned about the art of oratory comes from observing students and colleagues giving their academic and professional presentations, but I also want to acknowledge the authors listed in the Further Reading section at the end of this book, whose works provided me with inspiration, perspective, and corroboration.

Thanks are also due the editorial and production departments at PPI for all the hard work that contributed to the publication of this book. I am especially grateful to Marjorie R. Roueche, acquisitions editor, for starting the whole process; to Scott Marley, for his skill, diligence, and patience in editing the manuscript; and to production manager Cathy Schrott, compositor Kate Hayes, and illustrator Amy Schwertman.

Finally, thanks to my late husband Van, who was my most important role model, and to my son E.J., who makes everything wonderful and worthwhile.

Introduction

Here you are with some pretty good ideas to convey—maybe even great ones. But the thought of giving a presentation is making you nervous and insecure. Like many others, you have given speechmaking the top spot on your list of Least Agreeable Things to Do.

But you also know that scientific, engineering, and business presentations can be costly when done poorly, and important and valuable when done skillfully. Employees who can do them well are usually highly prized. Most companies, including many on the Fortune 500, have placed public speaking at the top of their lists of Valued Professional Proficiencies.

Fortunately, you have some natural abilities to draw upon, and you can tap into them readily. After all, the human race has probably been making oral presentations of one kind or another for hundreds of thousands of years. We all can be naturals at oratory to varying degrees; some of us just need a little extra training. Once you start drawing upon your communication genes, you will soon discover that presentation skills can be developed with relative ease. Release your "Inner Orator" and you too will be expressing your ideas effectively and persuading others to accept them.

The results are well worth the effort. Consider these questions:

Would you like to be the one whose name comes immediately to mind when new opportunities—jobs, promotions, and higher responsibilities—are offered?

Would you rather prepare and present your talks with efficiency, impact, and zest instead of frustration, anxiety, and embarrassment?

Would you like to receive full credit and recognition for those good ideas and discoveries that have emerged from your many long, hard hours of R&D?

You may have carefully cultivated a wide range of scientific knowledge and technical skills. But you still need another level of skill if you are to reach your full potential as a professional. Whatever professional goal you are pursuing—obtaining an advanced degree, a new position, or a promotion; winning a proposal, a government contract, professional recognition, or even a Nobel Prize—its achievement may depend not only on your technical skills but also on your presentation skills.

This book is aimed at helping you develop high-performance speaking skills that you will use every day, in situations ranging from short, informal meetings to full-scale conference presentations. It stresses the cause-and-effect relationship between how well you present and how readily your audience accepts what you say.

ALL THE WORKPLACE IS A STAGE

You are probably well aware that business and technical professionals are frequently called upon to perform—to present their ideas out loud. You are in some respects on a professional stage, whether you are making a simple phone call or presenting a formal talk at a conference podium. And like an actor in the theater, you too must make yourself seen and heard, you must be convincing, and you must connect to the minds of your audience.

You must cultivate effective performance techniques, therefore, just as conscientiously as you have cultivated your scientific, mathematical, and technical skills. For just as a weak performance by an actor can ruin the best play, a weak performance on the professional stage can obscure a useful idea or sink a worthwhile project.

You must also be a very versatile speaker. The range and variety of on-the-job presentations are enormous—laboratory and project reports, trip debriefings, conference papers, presentations to committees and clients, equipment and procedure demonstrations, and employee training sessions, to name just a few. The scientist, architect, engineer, or technical professional who has also achieved some mastery of presentation techniques clearly has the advantage.

MANY REASONS TO SPEAK

Consider some typical situations that young professionals might face.

A quality control consultant must deliver a training program for a federal agency so that workers can learn what the techniques of statistical process control are and how they can put these and other standard quality measures into practice.

During an eight-month stay in Japan, an engineering intern worked on electric power storage in semi-conductors for a Tokyo firm. He had to present frequent progress report sessions, which often turned into open forums for evaluation and discussion. Now back at the university, he must discuss his experiences with fellow students and faculty advisors at a graduate seminar.

Two seniors at Keystone Tech must collaborate on an oral presentation of their senior design project, a new design for an antenna test facility. They will speak to an audience composed of faculty evaluators and other graduate students.

After the successful completion of his master's degree at Garden State University, a young engineer begins his first big job at Universal Electronics Laboratories, working on state-of-the-art technology in microwave-photonic technology. After only six months in his new job, he achieves some remarkable results; consequently, he is called upon to present them to management.

An architect must explain and demonstrate the working of a new HVAC installation to coworkers and customers. She expects some heated arguments over certain unexpected air-conditioning costs. She realizes that she needs to achieve an excellent performance if she is to convince an audience prejudiced against cost overruns.

At a professional conference, an oceanographer will present his findings on the use of underwater lasers to map the ocean bottom. His audience will include 30 to 40 engineers, who will be sure to ask in-depth questions.

And so the list goes on...

THE PRICE OF POOR PRESENTATIONS

Business professionals generally understand they need good presentation skills. Ideas and products do not simply sell themselves. These professionals have been trained to value salesmanship.

But scientists, engineers, and other technical professionals sometimes put their faith in their content alone to sell their ideas. The realization that they must make a real effort to develop good presentation technique often comes as a surprise—even a shock.

Some of this tendency to ignore presentation skills lies in simple dread. Many people have an exaggerated fear of making oral presentations—whether formal or informal, long or short—so that they go to great lengths to avoid speaking in public and ignore their need to develop as speakers. The result is that the professional world is filled with weak, inadequate presentations.

Now imagine if we were to calculate the cost of all the ineffectual, disorganized, and boring presentations that occurred over the last year. The cost in wasted employee hours and missed opportunities would be enormous.

PRESENTATION SKILLS ARE POWER TOOLS

Fortunately, public speaking is not an inborn talent bestowed on a favored few. It can be learned—and so with some thought and practice, you too can design and develop presentations that achieve your purpose and satisfy the informational needs of your audience. You can learn to present your ideas with efficiency and confidence.

Think of oral communication as a craft, and your presentation skills and techniques as a special set of tools—powerful and practical tools that you, as a craftsperson, can learn to use with ever increasing effectiveness, as you build your career success and make your mark on the world of work.

Your ability to acquire and use these tools can bring you all sorts of favorable attention in the workplace. Whether a student or a seasoned professional, you can benefit from improving your speaking skills—simply because you will be called on to speak so frequently.

Good speaking skills make you stand out from the ranks of mediocre speakers. Professional audiences tend to be composed of reasonably intelligent people, who certainly do not appreciate a boring talk. As some very accomplished researchers have discovered, even a brilliant concept will fail to shine because of a dull presentation. If you want to show your great ideas in the best light, now is the time to start polishing your presentation tools.

THE CRAFT OF THE TECHNICAL PRESENTATION

Just like good technical writing, good technical reporting relies on knowing how to structure, develop, and present your ideas so that they will make sense to your listeners. An oral presentation demands the same sense of planning and purpose, the same level of audience awareness, and the same attention to detail that a written report demands.

Some important differences are apparent, however, because your communication medium is different.

Your vocal expression and your gestures and movement, aided by visuals and selected equipment, will affect the listener in a different way than the printed page does the reader.

While a reader may skim, skip around, and reread a written report, your listeners must absorb information in a linear way. A spoken message must flow through time and is always time dependent. When you present an oral report, therefore, you need to take these differences into consideration at all stages, from the planning to the presentation of the talk.

GIVING INFORMAL PRESENTATIONS

In a typical workday you will have many occasions to communicate informally with supervisors, coworkers, vendors, and customers. Every improvement that you make in your speaking skills, therefore, will reward you abundantly and frequently.

You could be called on to make short (under 15 minutes) and informal presentations.

Oral briefings. Your supervisor may ask you to give a short informative talk, perhaps about your laboratory results, a new procedure, or a company policy. A technical briefing is usually a short progress report about your work.

Instructions. You may have to explain a task to other engineers or technicians who are working with you on a project.

Committee reports. You may be asked to give a brief presentation at a meeting. You may have a mixed audience of managers and technical personnel.

Telephone calls. You will frequently have to call clients, colleagues, customers, and vendors. Often, you will leave a voicemail message.

Even the most informal situation can yield better results if you take the time for the following simple rules.

- Define your purpose.
- Think about the informational needs of the audience.
- Sketch out a brief outline and make some informal notes.
- Limit your content to highlights or key points.
- Remember that you do not have time for many details.

GIVING FORMAL PRESENTATIONS

But these short talks aren't all. As a technical professional, you are likely to be called sooner or later to give a formal presentation. You may need to deliver a paper at a conference, or present a proposal at a meeting. This sort of event can be even more challenging than presenting an informal talk to your coworkers. Your audience's expectations are different, and you may be less at ease because the situation is more formal. Your surroundings are unfamiliar, and the audience will be larger.

How do you prepare? Here's the temptation: Just read your paper directly from your published version. Use a dull monotone.

Result: Your audience goes to sleep. Or they sneak out when they notice you aren't looking because your eyes are buried in your paper.

Listeners take in information differently than readers do. That means you have to take a different approach. You will need these things for a successful formal presentation.

- a thorough analysis of your purpose, audience, and situation
- a careful preparation of content and visual support
- a structure for your report that is both appropriate and effective
- plenty of practice

WHAT THIS BOOK CONTAINS

The chapters of this book will focus on different aspects of giving presentations, both formal and informal.

Chapter 1 will help you plan and develop the content and organization of your presentation.

Chapter 2 shows how to design visual aids that will best support that content.

Chapter 3 tells how to manage and handle various types of visual support.

Chapter 4 stresses the importance of strong delivery techniques. It will show you how to improve your skills so you can deliver your material with clarity, conviction, and maximum effectiveness.

Chapter 5 warns against traps and pitfalls to avoid when preparing and presenting a talk.

Chapter 6 tests you on what you've learned. Be prepared. Be very prepared.

The techniques and guidelines in these chapters will help you improve the skills and build on the experience you already have as a speaker. With practice, you can learn to present your ideas with confidence, so that your listeners will accept them and remember them long after you have left the podium.

1

Preparing Your Oral Presentation

Grasp the subject – the words will follow.

—Cato the Elder

Let's take a look at the most common preparation pitfalls.

Weak speakers too often make themselves ineffective by

- trying to cover too much, discussing every aspect, or including every detail
- focusing on their own interests and forgetting about what the audience wants to learn
- assuming that ease and naturalness will come without practice

Now let's look at some ways of avoiding these pitfalls.

CLARIFY YOUR PURPOSE

What is your fundamental goal? The first step is to think about your underlying objective. This step may seem obvious, yet many speakers start preparing their presentations with only a vaguely conceived idea *to write something about something*. No wonder so many presentations are poorly organized—they have no clear central point.

To help you focus on your purpose, ask yourself these questions.

> *Why am I making this particular presentation?*
>
> *What am I trying to accomplish?*
>
> *What do I want people to do after they read my report or hear my presentation?*

Here are some good questions for focusing on what you want.

> *Do I simply want to present a set of data? Or do I need to manipulate the data in some way: to define, to compare, to categorize?*
>
> *Am I trying to change anything? To elicit certain actions or reactions?*
>
> *Is my intention to sell a product? To persuade my audience to accept a new process or an innovative idea? To commission my company's services?*

Your objectives will often involve one or more of these basic intentions.

- to inform
- to persuade
- to recommend
- to teach or train
- to warn

- to activate
- to sell
- to solicit approval
- to honor
- to accept an honor

Carefully define your purpose before you begin to develop your talk. This step will help ensure your success with every other part of the process. With your intentions clear, you can select and organize your materials so that every aspect of your presentation furthers your objectives.

A strong, clear statement of purpose makes a solid foundation for your communication. Starting out with an informal "I want to…" can lead to a well-focused purpose statement.

Another good technique is to use a strong, active-voice verb phrase as the heart of your statement. "I *intend to convince* the Board of Directors that we need to increase the equipment budget."

BUILD ON AN UNDERLYING IDEA

Closely related to your purpose statement is the underlying idea that supports your entire presentation. This is the message that emerges directly from your purpose. *Upgrading our equipment will help us increase productivity and customer satisfaction.*

Before developing your talk, be sure to have both your purpose and your central idea clearly defined for yourself in writing. Then, as you develop your supporting points, make sure that everything supports your purpose and pertains directly to your central idea.

Sometimes you can't even determine your key point until you're clear on what it is you're trying to do. Here's a simple exercise that can help you define your objectives and plan your approach.

1. Write down the topic of your talk. Define the topic as explicitly and clearly as you can in one affirmative sentence.
2. Circle the words in this statement that indicate your key points.
3. Add any additional words that come to mind.
4. Use these key ideas as the basis for your outline.

HIT THE HIGH POINTS

A good talk can't cover everything. Say too much and you may lose your audience. A written report can go into deep detail, but an oral report on the very same project can make only a few points and still be clear to the listener.

So as you plan your oral presentation, don't include every last point you could present. Focus on the key issues.

Here's a step-by-step method of keeping your material under control. It works well for all presentations, informal and formal. You could use this method to plan a briefing or an informal presentation, or to extract key information from a paper that you have already written.

1. *Find the key point.* If your listeners come away from your talk having learned only one thing, what would you want it be? Write this sentence in bold letters at the top of your planning sheet or computer file. Refer to it often as you develop your presentation.

2. *List the supporting points that you consider very important.* Leave space between them for additions or reorganization.

3. *Look at your list again.* Consider all your points. Do some of them now seem unnecessary, redundant, or less important than the others? Cross them out.

4. *Highlight the points that you think will interest your audience.* This step will be useful later when you develop the slides or other visual support for the talk.

5. *Determine how many points you can hit in the time you have.* Develop the discussion for several of them. How long does it take? This will give you an idea of how much you can really cover in the time allotted to you. Surprisingly, you're more likely to have too much material than not enough.

6. *Select your most important points.* There's a little wiggle room either way, but it's usually better to have too few points rather than too many.

7. *Find the best order for presenting your points.* It doesn't have to be the same order as in your written report. Listeners often need a different approach than readers do. Number your points in the order you'll present them.

Now you have the beginnings of a strong outline for your presentation.

CONSIDER THE NEEDS OF YOUR AUDIENCE

Many speakers spend a lot of time preparing the content of their talks, but neglect one of the best ways to ensure a successful presentation: careful consideration of the needs of their audience. Take time to think about what information your audience wants and needs and you'll put yourself at a clear advantage.

Your presentation is really a cooperative effort between you and your audience. A successful talk needs a receptive audience. You therefore need to find ways to engage them in listening effectively. A good speaker makes a very careful analysis of the audience.

Exercise: Analyzing Your Audience
Consider these questions about your audience.

Who are they? What is their relationship to you?

- ☐ customers
- ☐ supervisors
- ☐ subordinates
- ☐ fellow experts or peers
- ☐ trainees
- ☐ clients and customers

What do they want from you?

- ☐ information
- ☐ analysis
- ☐ solutions and recommendations
- ☐ alternatives

What do you want from them?

- ☐ understanding
- ☐ acceptance of your ideas
- ☐ approval of a project
- ☐ approval of funding
- ☐ change of attitude or behavior

☐ decision on alternatives

☐ improved performance

What are the physical conditions affecting your audience?

☐ size of group

☐ distance from speaker

☐ hunger or fatigue

These questions will help you adjust your content to the informational needs of your audience and ensure that your presentation thoroughly engages them.

REVIEW THE SETTING FOR YOUR PRESENTATION

You are at an advantage if you can review the physical layout—that is, the scene for your presentation—even before you start developing your talk. In that way, you can plan for ways both to surmount problems and to adapt your presentation to the physical surroundings to your best advantage.

Exercise: Analyzing the Setting
Consider the following questions.

The room

☐ What size is it?

☐ Are its acoustics good?

☐ Are the lines of vision adequate?

☐ How many seats are there? Can they be moved?

☐ Can your audience take notes? Are writing surfaces provided?

☐ Is the lighting good?

☐ Can the shades be drawn? How will you darken the room for projected visuals?

☐ Will the room tend toward being too hot or too cold?

☐ Can windows be opened and closed?

The speaker's equipment

☐ Will you have a podium?

☐ Will you have a table for materials and papers?

☐ Do you need to arrange for a microphone?

Audio-visual equipment

☐ What kind of projector is provided?

☐ Will you need help in setting up and operating it?

☐ Does the room already have a screen?

☐ Is there a chalkboard or whiteboard? A flip chart?

☐ Will you require chalk? A pointer?

☐ Is your presentation software compatible with the software provided?

A thorough review of the room and the equipment will help you feel more confident. If you have time, test your presentation on the equipment. Make sure equipment and software is functioning properly—well before the audience arrives.

It's also advisable to prepare for system failure or incompatibility, especially if you are presenting outside of your home office. You may bring your slide presentation in several formats, just in case something goes wrong. Here are some fail-safe methods.

- Bring enough hard copies of your slide presentation for everyone.
- Email your presentation to yourself for easy electronic retrieval.
- Carry along a mini-drive as a backup.

Be on your guard when using new technology. It can seduce you into trusting it too much—and then betray you.

CHOOSE YOUR MODE OF DELIVERY

Oral presentations are usually one or a combination of these basic types.

- the impromptu talk
- the memorized speech
- the manuscript talk
- the extemporaneous talk

Which presentation method should you select?

The Impromptu Talk

When you need to speak off the cuff, it's usually because you have no choice. Sometimes you'll find yourself in a speaking situation in which you've been given little or no preparation time. You may be called upon to speak at a conference or meeting, or you may need to respond to an unexpected question at the end of one of your prepared speeches.

Here are some tips for making impromptu talks work.

- Even if your preparation time is only a matter of minutes or even seconds, think before you speak. At least decide on the order in which you will present your ideas.
- If time allows, jot down a few notes on whatever is handy—a scrap of paper, a napkin—and try to sketch an informal outline.
- Take a deep breath, look your listeners in the eye, and begin.

The Memorized Speech

Unless you have occasion to present a poem or a quotation, or you want to convey some special idea in a memorable manner or establish a special mood, you probably should avoid memorization.

Sometimes an inexperienced speaker is tempted to write out and memorize a talk, because speaking extemporaneously seems too uncertain or frightening a proposition. But don't give in to this temptation.

There are definite disadvantages to this type of talk.

- You will need an enormous amount of time for memorization.
- Unless you are a consummate actor, you will probably sound mechanical and thus lose rapport with your audience.
- Your mind may go blank. Missing a word or reversing an idea may cause the whole structure of your talk to collapse.

There are only a few times when you really should opt for memorizing. You may need to give some standard presentation for the company, such as a welcoming speech or a guided tour of the facility. Otherwise, steer clear of memorizing anything more than just short parts of your talk.

The Manuscript Talk

Occasionally, you may need to read your talk from a written text. This is the typical means of presenting material when you must be highly accurate or precise—for example, in a situation involving sensitive legalities. Many presentations at engineering and scientific conferences and symposia are given in this manner.

But this method can be problematic. If you read your paper in a monotone or without adequate preparation, the audience may heartily wish they had picked up a reprint and stayed in their hotel rooms, instead of sitting on an uncomfortable folding chair, listening to you mumble and drone.

Most people have difficulty making a manuscript talk sound natural. This is probably because speech and writing are quite different in style. But by preparing carefully and then calling upon your acting skills, you can produce a performance that will engage and hold your audience's interest.

What can you do to make this kind of presentation effective?

- Print a copy of your talk in larger print. This task is easy to do with a word processor. The resulting script will let you to look away from the page and to maintain better audience contact.
- Break each sentence into the cadences of normal and graceful speech. This helps you to speak naturally and to avoid becoming monotonous.

- Leave ample white space between the lines and paragraphs. This will help you keep your place without gluing your eyes to the page.

- Use notations in the text in parentheses and capitals, like (PAUSE) or (LOOK AT AUDIENCE) to remind yourself where you want to place special emphasis.

- Use highlighters or colored pens to underline important ideas or emphasize key points. These can also remind you where you wanted to add emphasis.

- If possible, obtain a lectern so that your script is closer to your eyes and your hands are free for an occasional gesture. Be sure you have adequate lighting so that you don't have to bury your face in the script. Remember that the audience will find your face more interesting than the top of your head.

- Practice. Try reading expressively in front of a mirror or into a tape recorder. Watch out for falling into a monotone or a sing-song voice. If you can face yourself—probably your toughest critic—you'll be better prepared to face others.

The Extemporaneous Talk

Most experienced speakers prefer to speak extemporaneously—that is, from notes rather than from a script. This type of presentation aims at a conversational and natural style, yet it is quite different from the impromptu (off-the-cuff) talk.

The distinction lies in the level of preparation and practice. The extemporaneous talk is usually supported by carefully designed visual aids.

You will speak only from notes or an outline and stop short of memorization. A well-done extemporaneous presentation seems natural and conversational, and must never seem stiff or "canned." The level of interaction of speaker and audience is high. The speaker must have all his or her ideas clearly thought out, but the exact choice of words occurs as the talk goes on.

Use the following method to prepare for an extemporaneous talk.

- Familiarize yourself thoroughly with your subject. You will need to be very knowledgeable if your presentation is to be both interesting and smooth.

- Consider your audience, so that you can anticipate which aspects of the subject will best hold their interest.

- Develop an outline that best suits your purpose, audience, and situation. You may use it to help you remember enough of the necessary points and details of your report.

- Use an extra set of slides or some 4 × 6 note cards to serve as speaker's notes. Be sure to number them, just in case you drop them while you're speaking.

- Practice the talk until you feel at ease with it, but stop before completely committing it to memory. In your performance, you want to sound so familiar with your material that the ideas flow naturally and easily.

2

The Main Parts of Your Talk

Think of a presentation as a dialog in which the audience grants you permission to speak first.

—Cliff Atkinson

An oral presentation usually has three main parts: the introduction, the body or discussion, and the conclusion.

Simpler in structure than a formal written report, an oral presentation is typically organized somewhat like those five-paragraph "keyhole" essays you may have been assigned back in English class. For those who don't remember, a keyhole essay consists of an opening paragraph that introduces a specific theme, several paragraphs that develop the theme, and a closing paragraph that connects the theme with more general issues.

This format works well for business and technical presentations. It has particular appeal for American audiences who favor its direct structure: a clear beginning, middle, and end. Of course, the way you develop the central part of the talk depends upon its purpose. For example, an argument, a proposal, and

13

a technical briefing would each have its own distinctive pattern of development. (Chapter 3 will go into more detail on this point.)

A presentation may also have an optional fourth part: the question-and-answer period.

Your listeners will expect a concise presentation, organized to fit its purpose. Each of these parts needs careful preparation.

Figure 2.1. The Keyhole Structure

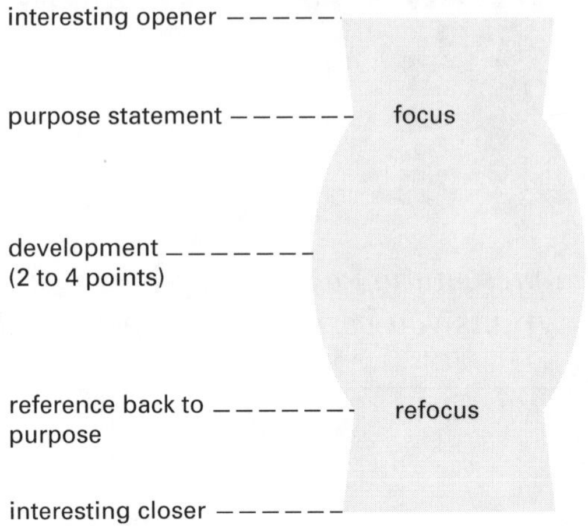

interesting opener — — — — —

purpose statement — — — — — —   focus

development _ _ _ _ _ _ _
(2 to 4 points)

reference back to _ _ _ _ _ _ _   refocus
purpose

interesting closer — — — — — —

THE INTRODUCTION

Your opening is crucial to your presentation. You need to arouse your listeners' interest and curiosity, impress upon them the importance of your subject, and convince them of the worth of your ideas as well as your knowledge and understanding of the material. Keep the length of your introduction in proportion with your talk, usually no more than 10% of the whole.

You need to accomplish several tasks in the introduction.

- ☐ Introduce yourself and your subject.
- ☐ Define your purpose and scope explicitly.
- ☐ Capture the audience's interest.

A good introduction responds to most or all of the following questions—unless the answers are already known to everyone in your audience.

- ☐ Who are you?
- ☐ What are your credentials and qualifications?
- ☐ What is your specific topic, and how is it restricted?
- ☐ Why are you presenting this topic?
- ☐ How is this topic relevant to the interests of your audience?
- ☐ What general approach are you taking to your topic and how is it divided?

Here are some ways to involve your audience.

State the problem. Describe the problem, then suggest a solution.

Offer an interesting fact. Say something that may surprise or amuse the audience.

Tell them a story. Begin with a short narrative, serious or humorous, that bears on the subject of your talk. Everyone loves a story, and this technique allows you to spark the audience's interest and put them at ease at the same time. You may want to use an actual incident that relates to your subject. If you use a hypothetical story, be sure to clearly designate it as such.

Give them some numbers. Put your subject into an interesting perspective by presenting statistics. Take care to relate the statistics carefully to your purpose, as mere numbers have a way of becoming confusing. *Over the next decade, we will see a 300% increase in the number of applications for...*

Open with a pertinent quotation. A memorable saying can capture your listeners' interest and help them remember the point of your talk. Your talk on new technology might open with a classic quotation. *Samuel Johnson once said, "Everything is possible with diligence and skill."* Or you might cite a current expert in the field. *According to Peter K. Gigahertz, president of Specialty Electronics, the electric cord as we know it may soon be obsolete, thanks to new developments in large fiber technology.*

THE BODY OR DISCUSSION

The body will be the longest section of your talk. Here is where you present the details that support your major points.

There are many ways to organize material; some basic ways are listed here. You may use one of them alone or combine more than one. For example, the main organizing principle for your talk may be *problem and solution*. But you may use *analysis* and *comparison and contrast* in the development of the subsections.

Chronology. Use the order in which something is done or in which events occurred.

Analysis. Examine an object, a process, or a concept by considering its component parts.

Categorizing. Arrange ideas or information in logical and useful groups.

Comparison and contrast. Highlight similarities and differences.

Investigation of alternatives. Examine and compare several alternative solutions.

Process description. Analyze a procedure or occurrence step by step.

Object or device description. Focus on physical attributes.

Problem and solution. Set up a set of criteria against which you will measure your selected solution.

Question and answer. Pose a question and provide an answer or an evaluation of alternative answers.

Cause and effect. Trace the source of some problem, and show what effects some course of action would have.

Topics or concepts. Show criteria such as analysis, testing, evaluation, application.

Journalistic style. Tell *who, what, why, where, when.*

Deductive argument. Demonstrate *if, then, therefore.*

Advertising. Use this business-world method, which is sometimes called AIDA (Attention-Interest-Desire-Appeal)

Summary. Provide an overview or summing up of the most important points.

In all cases, fit your organizing mode to the interests and informational needs of the audience. Don't present a detailed chronological narrative of how you solved a problem if your listeners are interested in learning why one solution to a problem is superior to another. Don't present a long technical description if your audience of managers is interested in cost control methods and new applications.

Listeners, Not Readers

Be careful to maintain a view of your audience as *listeners* rather than *readers*. You need to make your organization very clear to them. They will not process your material in the same way that readers of a written report would.

Readers can jump from section to section in any order, reread sections they don't understand, zero in on the parts they're interested in, and skim or even skip over the parts they're not. Chapter headings and subheadings help them understand how your report is organized even before they begin to read.

Listeners must approach your material linearly, in the order you present it. If they're confused by a sentence or a whole section, they can't go back and hear it again. And they don't have a guide to the overall structure of your presentation, unless you help them out.

Therefore, you need to make a number of adjustments in your approach to compensate for the slow, linear way that the spoken word reaches your audience.

Here are some helpful tips.

Slim down your talk to the essentials. Make your speech "lean and mean." Include only the background that your particular audience needs.

Plan appropriate visuals. This practice is essential for technical or numerical material. Good visuals will lessen the need for excessive verbiage and add impact and clarity.

Provide signals within your report. Enumerate major points and lists by indicating order. Designate chronological sequences, make points of comparison obvious, and clarify hierarchies.

Use strong transitions. Your listeners need to follow your thought, maintain concentration, and remember your main points. Highlight the direction of your ideas and tie each section of your talk together with what has preceded and what will follow.

Comment on the material. Point out what is particularly important or interesting. Stress the key points that the audience needs to notice and remember.

Repeat—with discretion—your major points. Example: "This new system will save over half of the communication budget. Yes, that's close to 60%." But be careful not to repeat yourself so much that you become tiresome.

Supply mini-summaries within the talk itself. When you finish a section or wind up a point, provide a one-line review of what you have just covered. This recap can also help you develop an effective coherence between sections.

THE CONCLUSION

In your technical reporting, you may have learned to put all the important materials at the beginning. This is because of the way technical reports are read, with most attention given to the opening sections like the abstract, executive summary, and introduction. Even recommendations and conclusions are frequently placed right after the introduction because many readers, particularly executives, won't read the report from cover to cover.

One major difference between a written report and an oral report, therefore, is that an oral presentation demands a really impressive conclusion, in much the same way an essay does. Even if you have already mentioned the final outcome of your argument—for example, you may have mentioned in your introduction what your solution to the problem will be—you will want to state it again at the end. The ending of your talk plays a dynamic role in the success of your whole presentation.

How do you make an ending memorable? It must

- establish your major points firmly in the minds of your audience
- bring your presentation to a fitting and memorable close

You can close your presentation effectively, therefore, by including a quick summary of the salient points covered in the body. This will imprint your points in your listeners' minds.

Human beings are subject to rapid short-term memory loss, but when material is repeated in an interesting way, it has a much better chance of being placed into long-term memory. This is the effect you desire. You should refer back to the purpose indicated in your introduction and be sure you have clarified your major points. A good way to do this is with a summary visual, but be sure that it is interesting summary rather than just a dry recap.

Finally, you should end with a significant closing remark that rounds out your presentation emphatically and memorably. Just what this closing is depends upon your purpose, audience, situation, and any of the other variables relating to your presentation.

Try developing several of these closing techniques for your talk.

- Recommend a change or a new course of action.
- Offer a prediction.
- Issue a challenge—a call for future action.
- Make a judgment.
- Present an interesting paradox.
- Make a specific request for approval.
- Suggest an application.
- Cite a surprising statistic.
- End with a pertinent quotation.

Then choose the best of these to add some real interest to your closing.

Carefully plan your very last word or phrase. Too often, speakers run out of energy and mumble, "Well, that's all I have to say," or "I guess that's about it."

Instead, prepare to end with a bang, not a whimper—and be sure that that statement ends on a strong word or phrase. Examples: *future, success, significantly higher profits, employee satisfaction, productivity.*

THE QUESTION-AND-ANSWER PERIOD

One advantage that the speaker has over the writer is the opportunity for immediate feedback. You can clarify points your audience may have understood poorly and can amplify them as needed.

The question-and-answer period that typically follows the conclusion provides an excellent opportunity for an active interchange between speaker and audience. The way to prepare is to anticipate the questions that the audience might ask and have some answers ready.

Don't worry if you don't know the answer to every question. Simply admit it and tell the questioner that you will have to look into that question more deeply. Make a note of the question and plan to discuss it later.

3

Designing Effective Visual Support

Power corrupts. PowerPoint corrupts absolutely.

—Edward Tufte

Visuals can often convey ideas and information in ways that words alone cannot. Consequently, visual support has become an important part of scientific, engineering, and technical presentations.

When preparing a presentation, you can choose from many options in developing visuals: anything from a quick sketch on the chalkboard to a detailed architectural model or multimedia display. But whatever form your visuals take, they must work toward the purpose of your report. Like any well-designed and well-engineered device, their output must justify their input. If not, your presentation will be better off without them.

Well-designed visuals can enhance your presentation in many ways.

Good visuals help focus your audience's attention. The human mind loves to wander, and your listeners' thoughts can readily drift to other concerns—deals in the making, recent arguments, plans for the weekend, even upcoming presentations of their own. Fortunately, good visuals will draw the eye, capture the interest, and help keep the mind on track.

Good visuals encourage memory retention. We tend to remember visual impressions much more easily than verbal content. We also hold on to information better when we take it in through more than one sense. Visuals can simplify complex ideas and relationships; those listeners who may miss a point presented verbally may understand it readily when it is presented through an interesting illustration or graph. Thus, combining visual impact with your verbal message can help your listeners remember your message long after the talk is over.

Good visuals emphasize, clarify, and augment your key points. A talk typically includes two to four key points, each of which needs at least one slide clearly stating it, along with as many others as are necessary to develop it. When your key points need additional proof or explanation, pictures, graphics, statistics, telling quotations, comparison charts, and concrete examples can add support to what you have to say.

Good visuals make you more persuasive. Poor visuals can make you look less sure of what you're saying. If your visuals look professional and technically sound, you'll appear more knowledgeable and in command of your material.

THE VARIETY OF VISUAL SUPPORT

Your choice of visuals is limited only by resources you have available. Your visuals can be cheap or expensive, static or dynamic, purely symbolic or the actual object itself.

But whatever the choices available to you, you should select your visual support by how appropriate and useful it is in getting your message across. Use visuals freely, but don't let the technology get in the way. Too much dazzle will distract the audience from your point.

In visual design, less is often more.

Now let's consider the various types of visual aids and equipment that speakers like to use.

With a projector

- slides and transparencies
- opaque projector visuals
- photos, pictures, and illustrations
- films and videos
- high-tech visual support

On the wall

- chalkboards and whiteboards
- flip charts

In your hands

- physical objects
- handouts

The computer-generated slide show, supplemented by handouts, is the most common form of visual support nowadays, and it's probably the one you'll use most often. This chapter is therefore focused on slides and handouts, but much of the advice here can be applied to other kinds of visuals as well.

PLANNING YOUR VISUAL CONTENT

As a general rule, you should plan your visual support even before you develop the spoken part of your presentation.

The more of your message you can get across visually, the greater the impact it will make on your audience. They will remember it better, too, so you want to focus your energies on this phase.

Planning your visuals first is usually more efficient as well. Once your visuals are developed, your words will flow more naturally around them. What's more, you will probably need fewer words than you thought you did. As a rule, an effective visual is worth about four minutes of speaking time.

So how should a speaker determine what visual content to include?

Some speakers use a storyboard in the early stages of planning and creating a talk. A storyboard is a technique derived from the way scripts are developed in the film industry. The talk is developed on one side of the page—either written in full or just outlined—with corresponding visuals sketched out at the appropriate points.

Figure 3.1. Storyboard

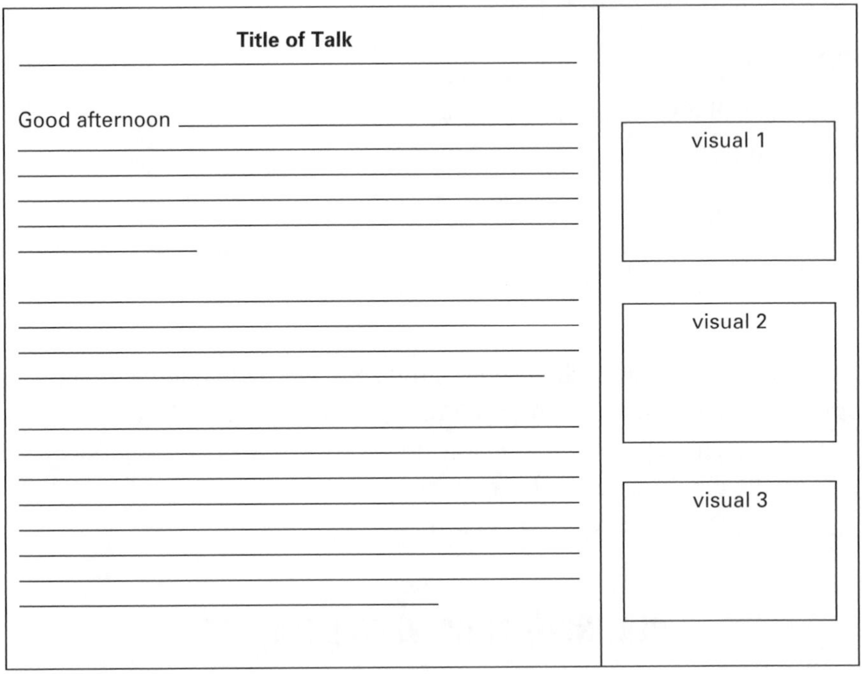

Title of Talk	
Good afternoon _____	visual 1
	visual 2
	visual 3

A storyboard helps you coordinate your talk and your visual support.

DEVELOPING THE COMPUTER-GENERATED SLIDE SHOW

If you have even modest computer skills, you can develop slides for your talk with presentation software such as PowerPoint. Most of these programs have an outlining feature that will let you develop your content and slides concurrently, in much the same way as a storyboard does. Each slide will become an organic part of your report, with a real purpose to serve, and not just an afterthought.

These programs also make it easy to design your slides, offering you a number of prepared layouts and styles that you can put your content into. Giving your slides visual variety will help your audience stay attentive. The same software can also be used to develop overhead transparencies, as well as the corresponding handouts and note pages.

Most slides fall into three categories.

- *verbal*: words, sentences, bullet lists
- *pictorial*: photographs, drawings, maps, graphs, diagrams
- *mathematical*: numbers, statistics, formulas

Many slides, of course, combine two or more of these elements.

VERBAL SLIDES

You can occasionally use a full sentence on a slide, but verbal slides are often composed of bullet lists. These are easy to create, and programs like PowerPoint offer a range of interesting ways to arrange the words.

But because they're so easy, the temptation is to rely too fully on this kind of slide. Don't. A monotonous series of bullet lists will bore your audience. Retain their enthusiasm and interest by using other styles of slides wherever you can.

When you do use a verbal slide, take extra care to make it easy to read and correct in spelling and grammar. Make sure that items in a bullet list are parallel in hierarchy and grammatical form. Appropriate clip art can sometimes add interest.

Here are some guidelines for verbal slides.

- Keep words to a minimum.
- Exploit the impact of white space.
- Express parallel ideas with parallel grammatical structure.
- Use bullet lists sparingly, if at all.

- Limit lists to seven lines or fewer.
- Double-check grammar, spelling, and capitalization.

Figure 3.2. Verbal Slide

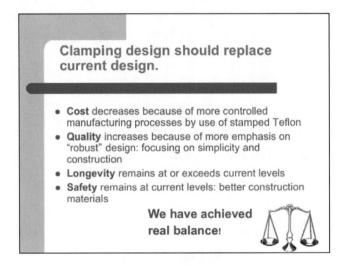

This verbal slide makes good use of clip art and white space.

(Courtesy of Wes Burns.)

PICTORIAL SLIDES

The best presentations, particularly for science and engineering, get their points across with graphs, tables, charts, photographs, maps, diagrams, and drawings.

When you use pictorial slides, audiences remember more of what you say. A photograph, for example, can save you many words, especially when you are trying to describe unusual or compelling physical conditions to your audience.

Here are some guidelines for pictorial slides.

- Make sure the picture is easy to see.
- Keep information to a minimum.
- Simplify as much as possible.

- Label important parts clearly.
- Add callouts or arrows to emphasize key points.
- Use color with good taste and discretion.

Figure 3.3. Photograph Slides

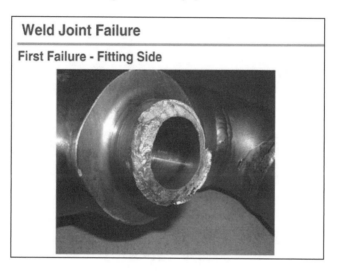

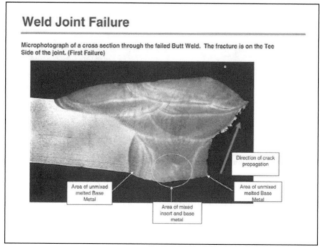

Two slides based on photographs.
Key points of interest are highlighted with labels and arrows.

(Courtesy of Anthony Leofsky.)

Figure 3.4. Chart Slides

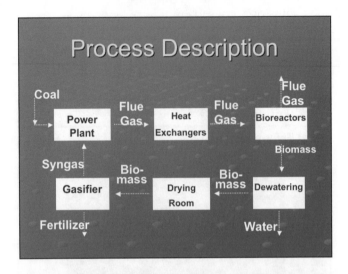

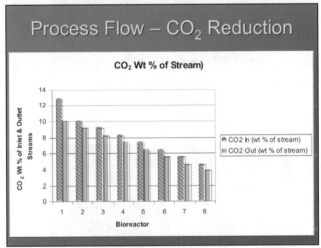

Two slides based on charts.
A program like PowerPoint can make these easy to prepare.

(Courtesy of Mohammed Baig.)

Figure 3.5. Diagram Slides

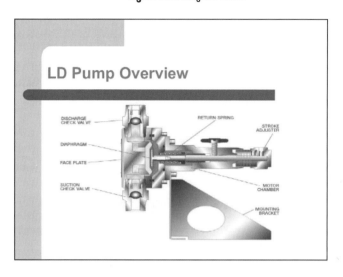

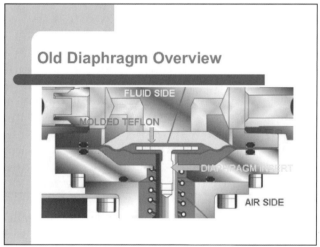

Two slides based on diagrams.

(Courtesy of Wes Burns.)

MATHEMATICAL SLIDES

Simplicity is especially important with mathematical content. If you're working with a lot of equations, a chalkboard or write-on transparency may be better than a slide projector. Your audience will find it easier to follow you as you work out a problem step by step on the board than to understand a long solution presented all at once on a slide.

Mathematical information is hard to read on slides. If you do use them, it's best to show only the key information. Anything more complicated—say, a long series of equations—should be distributed in a handout sheet.

Figure 3.6. Killer Mathematical Visual

$$
\begin{aligned}
P_l(\cos \gamma) &= \frac{4\pi}{2l + 1} \sum_{m=-l}^{l} (-1)^m Y_l^m \\
&\quad \times (\theta_1, \phi_1) Y_l^{-m}(\theta_2, \phi_2) \\
&= P_l(\cos \theta_1) P_l(\cos \theta_2) \\
&\quad + 2 \sum_{m=-l}^{l} \frac{(l-m)!}{(l+m)!} P_l^m(\cos \theta_2) \\
&\quad \times \cos(m(\phi_1 - \phi_2))
\end{aligned}
$$

A slide is a poor way of communicating complicated mathematical information.

Here are some guidelines for mathematical slides.

- Keep them as simple as possible.
- Make figures large enough to be read easily.
- Be generous with white space.
- Check scrupulously for accuracy.

Slides that look fussy or unprofessional can hurt the credibility of your presentation. No matter what type of visual you use, make sure it's clear, relevant, and appealing. Otherwise, leave it out.

Remember: In every case, simplicity is the rule.

Each part of the presentation—introduction, body, and conclusion—can be enhanced by visual support. Developing visuals for each part also helps you design and develop the whole presentation.

SUPPORTING THE OPENING

Your opening visuals need to support these important functions of a good introduction.

- introducing your topic
- previewing the content
- establishing your credibility
- generating audience interest and approval

Your opening slides should include the following two elements.

Title slide. Use one or more introductory slides to arouse your audience's interest, pique their curiosity, and impress them with the importance of your material. Your first slide should provide the title and date of your presentation and, of course, your name and affiliation. Make sure your title is interesting, and if possible add a subtitle that relates to your central idea. Including your credentials and your company's name and logo adds to your credibility. Adding a graphic or photograph will trigger interest on the part of the audience. Figure 3.7 shows how to create an engaging title slide.

Overview slide with key ideas. Complete the opening of your presentation with a concise list of the major points you plan to make. Listeners need all the help you can give them in focusing on your key ideas. But don't waste time here saying the obvious, or your audience's first impression may be that you're uninteresting—or worse, condescending.

Figure 3.7. Title Slides

(a) *Too minimal.*

(b) *Better but still not engaging.*

(c) *Informative and engaging.*

(Photo credit: Anthony Latess.)

Figure 3.8. Two Contrasting Overview Slides

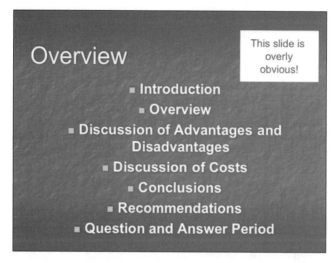

(a) an uninteresting overview

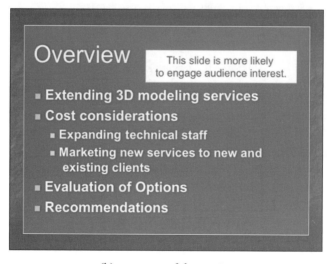

(b) a more useful overview

Another time-waster—and one all too often seen in scientific or engineering presentations—is the overcrowded slide. Too many words and too little white space can make even useful information seem overwhelming. Never force a slide to hold more information than it gracefully can.

Figure 3.9. Crowded Slide

Sponsored by Excello Electronics Laboratory
Objective: Development of optically phase/frequency cohered oscillators
Approach: Indirect subharmonic injection locked phase locked loop oscillator
Accomplishments:
• Analytic model of subharmonic injection locking in terms of nonlinear input-output characteristics off mmw devices
• Establishment of nonlinear current-voltage relation for FET, HEMT
• Design and fabrication of 6 GHz prototype oscillator for proof on concept study
• Load-pull measurement of 6 GHz oscillator
• Indirect subharmonic optical injection locking of 18 GHz oscillators
• Study phase coherency of 18 GHz oscillators
• Minimization of ILPLL circuit size and test of new concepts (to be completed by next year)

This slide is carrying excess baggage.

Aim for a reasonable balance in both content and spacing. Make your summary informative, but offer only enough information to give a useful and intelligible overview of the talk to come.

SUPPORTING THE BODY

Suppose you're giving your sales team some instruction on negotiating a deal involving your company's product. You might use a key-point slide, like the one in Fig. 3.10.

The slide needn't contain all the information. Its real purpose is to attract and focus your audience's attention. It therefore contains only a minimum of words; you supply the details as you explain and interpret it.

For developing the major points of your presentation, you can choose from the many types of slides we've already discussed. You can use purely verbal slides, pictorial slides of many kinds (photographs, drawings, tables, and more), mixed verbal/pictorial slides, and so on.

Remember: Don't get stuck in the bullet-list rut.

If you try to emphasize everything, nothing really stands out. Fire off one bullet-list slide after another and you'll quickly bore your audience.

Pictures have more impact than words, so help your audience with a presentation rich in graphics.

Another good principle:

Limit yourself to about one slide per minute of talk, and make each one count.

SUPPORTING THE CONCLUSION

An audience may have difficulty concentrating during an oral presentation. So you want to make an extra effort at the end to emphasize your central idea and key points one more time, and to leave your listeners with a favorable impression of what you have said. Ideally, your concluding slides and your handouts will accomplish these four functions.

- summarizing the important aspects of your presentation
- referring back to your central idea in an interesting way
- motivating the audience to respond in some way
- giving a sense of closure

A final slide that summarizes your key points can be useful. As always, keep words to a minimum.

Figure 3.10. Key-Point Slide

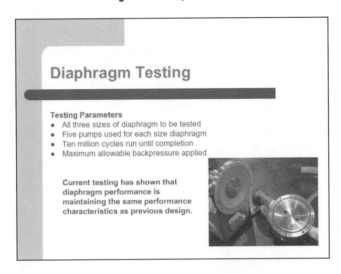

(Courtesy of Wes Burns.)

Figure 3.11. Slide with Arrow Callouts

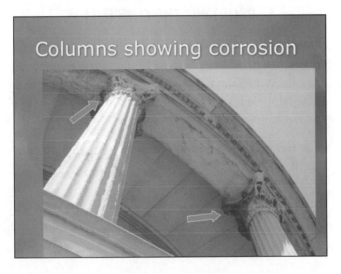

Emphasize pertinent information with arrow callouts.

(Photo credit: Anthony Latess.)

Figure 3.12. Slides with Labels and Arrows

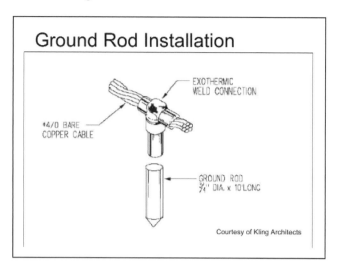

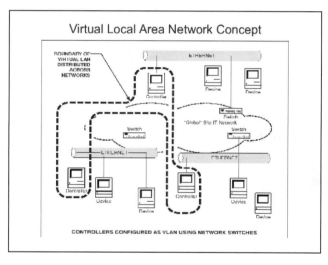

These two figures show how both simple and complex details are clarified with labels and arrows.

(Courtesy of Kling Architects.)

Figure 3.13. Large Schematic

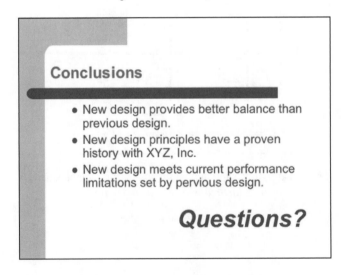

This graphic is too complicated to be read easily as a slide,
but once enlarged it could be displayed effectively on poster board.

(Courtesy of Kling Architects.)

Figure 3.14. Summary Slide

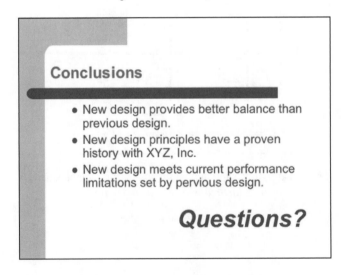

A slide like this can spark a good Q&A period.

(Courtesy of Wes Burns.)

You don't have to waste a whole slide just to announce your Q&A period. You may need to encourage your audience to ask questions, and a nearly blank slide with only the word "Questions?" on it may leave them staring back nearly as blankly.

A better idea is to add the word "Questions?" at the bottom of your summary slide (see Fig. 3.14). If you keep this slide in front of your audience after you finish speaking, it may help them remember your main points so that they can come up with good questions.

HANDOUTS

Nowadays it's a common courtesy to provide a set of handouts for your audience. A good set of handouts can be a powerful tool for impressing your message on the mind of a client or funder.

The easiest way to produce handouts is to copy your slides. The same software you developed your slides with will have an easy way to convert them to handouts, from one to nine slides per page. As you give your talk, your audience can make notes on the page that matches your slide.

You can also add comments to your slides. Using this feature, called "notes pages" in PowerPoint, can help you avoid a common mistake often seen in technical presentations: a slide packed with so much material so that the audience is quickly sent into a comatose state. Speakers are sometimes tempted to overload their slides so that their handouts, being printouts of the slides, will contain all the information they want their audience to carry away. Instead, keep your slides simple, and add the more detailed information to your notes pages. If you must leave behind complicated tables or mathematical data, provide these in hard-copy handouts. (In PowerPoint, you'll find this feature by pulling down the View menu and clicking on Notes.)

EVALUATING YOUR VISUAL SUPPORT

Effective visuals are crucial to the impact of your presentation. Studies have shown that, without good visual support, your audience may retain only 10%

to 20% of your talk once a few days have passed, while effective visuals can raise that figure to 60% to 70%.

When you prepare your talk, then, don't think of your visuals as optional, and don't develop them as an afterthought. Consider them an essential feature of your talk and give them sufficient planning, preparation, and practice.

No matter what types of visuals you plan to use—transparencies, computer-generated slides, physical objects, charts, photographs, handouts—they all need to meet the following standards.

Visibility. Make sure your audience, even those in the last row, can see everything. Is your lettering large enough to be read? Table 3.1 gives some guidelines.

Table 3.1. Font Sizes for Optimal Visibility

	headings	subheadings	text
PowerPoint slides and transparencies	36 pt	24 pt	18 pt
35 mm slides	24 pt	18 pt	14 pt
flip charts	4 in	2 in	1.5 in

But remember, the farther away your audience is, the larger the lettering needs to be. In very large rooms, increase the size so that even the people in the back rows can read your visuals easily.

Clarity. You want your audience to understand your message quickly and accurately. Therefore, clarity is essential in both text choices and slide design.

For clarity in text elements

- Use upper- and lowercase letters. Writing in all capitals is hard to read.
- Give simple lists of key words and ideas.
- Use parallel grammatical style to phrase express ideas.

For clarity in slide design and layout

- Keep contrast high between background and text.
- Refrain from placing text on a patterned background.
- Use arrows and labels to show what's important.
- Provide plenty of white space.

Simplicity. Overly complex slides will wear out your audience. Even intelligent and sophisticated listeners prefer a simple, straightforward message to a fussy, complicated, embellished one. For rapid comprehension, *less* usually works better than *more*.

- Limit each bullet list to seven lines or fewer.
- Use bullets, not asterisks, on your lists.
- Express your message in as few words as you can.
- When you can, use phrases instead of full sentences.
- Provide simple definitions for any unfamiliar terms.
- Prefer short words to long ones.

Consistency. Your presentation should have a generally consistent style throughout. Highlight your key ideas with a consistent design of headings and subheadings; label pictorial content in a consistent way.

- Be consistent in your font choices for headings and text.
- Avoid changing backgrounds or color schemes within a presentation.
- Readers read from left to right. Design your slides accordingly.

Presentation software can help you produce a well-designed set of slides and notes. Design a master slide to set your color scheme, font, and font size. You can also put a logo or other design element on every slide. The program will also have a variety of ready-made master slides you can use. Whether you choose one of these or design your own, opt for a more conservative design, not a flashy one. A design that calls attention to itself, with garish colors or unnecessary animation, can quickly become annoying as the presentation goes on.

Design your slides to help the reader's eye sweep over the information in the best way. We read from left to right, so take advantage of this habit by left-justifying your headings and text. This slide design will lead the eye from top left to bottom right, a reading pattern that will feel natural to your audience. An exception is your title slide, which often looks best centered.

Variety. A little variety can spark your audience's interest and help them remember key ideas.

- Use photographs and drawings to illustrate your points.
- Avoid relying too much on texts and bullet lists.
- Use animations or sounds only when they support your message.

Presentation software makes possible special effects in the transitions between slides. Be sparing as these can easily become annoying or distracting. Too much flash and your talk will crash.

Memory appeal. You can help your listener focus on your message and remember it better after the presentation is over by incorporating some simple mnemonic devices. If you use them, tailor them to your situation and your audience. A silly mnemonic might be perfect for an informal meeting but very wrong for a dignified international conference. See App. C for a mnemonics worksheet.

Aesthetic appeal. Your audience will respond to harmonious, balanced visuals. For example, don't use a new font on every slide; instead, limit yourself to one or two. A common choice is a sans serif font such as Arial for all your headings and a serif font such as Times for all your text. Sans serif fonts tend to be more pleasing to the eye, while serif fonts tend to be more readable. This gives your visuals some variety, but within a consistent design.

Choose an aesthetically pleasing color scheme that allows for excellent contrast between text and background. Use light text on a dark background, and dark text on a light background. Table 3.2 shows some standard combinations.

Your first concern should be to achieve high contrast for maximum readability. You can also use some bright colors, like red, for special accents, but use them very sparingly.

Table 3.2. Good Combinations of Background and Text Colors

background	headings	subheadings	text
navy, black, dark blue, or dark green	yellow, pale gold, or white	white	white or cream
white, cream, pale peach, or pale green	black, navy, dark green, or maroon	black, navy, or dark green	black

When designing your visual support,

- use the principles of consistency and variety to bring about a sense of harmony
- aim for balance in text, graphics, and white space

ASK FOR A VISUAL CRITIQUE

Before you present your talk, show your visuals to a colleague. Ask for feedback on their effectiveness in content and design. Then take a fresh look at them yourself.

When evaluating your presentation, be on the lookout for these visual villains.

- The Penny-Pincher: *Why use three slides when I can squeeze 500 words into one?*
- The Big Bore: *Maybe the audience won't notice how little I have to say.*
- The Fashion Flop: *Do fuchsia and chartreuse go together?*
- The Decorative Disaster: *If a little pizzazz is good, then a whole lot must be better.*
- The Masterpiece of Murk: *Dark lettering on a darker background— so subtle!*
- The Killer Equation: *This'll floor 'em—and they'll never get up!*

THE SOLUTION: CONSISTENCY, VARIETY, AND GOOD TASTE

A presentation should be consistent in its underlying design and structure. While the occasional surprising or eye-catching device can add emphasis and interest, an excess of visual impact could work against you, drawing your audience's attention away from your content. Therefore, when designing and selecting visual support, follow the Navy's well-known directive, KISS: Keep It Simple, Sailor!

But also follow that lesser-known but equally important principle, HUG, and make sure your visuals are

- Harmonious in style, color, and design
- Understandable at a glance
- Graphically rich

All in all, your audience will *love* your presentation if you let yourself be guided by these two helpful rules: KISS and HUG!

4

Managing and Handling Visual Support

The ability to simplify means to eliminate the unnecessary so that the necessary may speak.

—Hans Hofmann

Before you choose a certain type of visual, always consider its manageability. How hard will it be to transport? Could it fall over during the presentation? Will you have trouble manipulating it while you are speaking?

Imagine yourself handling the visual aid during the presentation. Even better, conduct a hands-on practice session. Then you can determine whether the effect is worth the trouble. Keep in mind that you must be able to use your visual support without inflicting any discomfort, boredom, or irritation on yourself or your listeners, or it will detract from your presentation. Evaluate every visual, therefore, to make sure that it really enhances your presentation.

Here's a preliminary checklist.

- ☐ Will this graphic offend the audience?
- ☐ Will it distract them?
- ☐ Is it garish or fussy?
- ☐ Is it so intrusive or cumbersome that it will interfere with the audience's concentration or with mine?
- ☐ Is it overly obvious, cluttered with information, or just plain boring?

If the answer to any of the above is yes, then revise the visual or leave it out.

- ☐ Is this slide really pertinent to the real purpose of the talk?
- ☐ Is this visual easy to see—even for those in the back of the room?
- ☐ Does this visual help the audience understand both the structure and the key points of the talk?
- ☐ Is the visual support elegant: satisfyingly neat, simple, tasteful, consistent, concise, and even ingenious?

If the answer to all of the above is yes, then leave it in!

GENERAL GUIDELINES FOR HANDLING VISUALS

You will build your credibility as a speaker if you handle your visual support with skill, ease, and grace. It's wise to design your visual support to be uncomplicated, and to test it carefully ahead of time. Here are some tips for addressing potential problems.

Pre-test informally. Use a *focus group* technique to test how your visuals will be received. Show them to others, perhaps some of your potential audience, and ask for feedback. Make sure your visuals do violate any cultural taboos or reveal any unauthorized confidential company data. When in doubt, ask someone who knows.

Practice your performance. If at all possible, arrange a "dress rehearsal" for yourself. Set up all equipment and materials ahead of time and run through the presentation. Practice with the equipment you will use to ensure that your subsequent talk will go smoothly and that all the equipment is working well.

You can also determine the best physical arrangement of the screen, the projector, and the podium so that you won't be blocking any audience member's view.

Coordinate your discussion with your visuals. Your audience may need time to look at a more complex visual. Stop talking and give them a few moments. If you have the right number of visuals (usually one per minute of your talk), you won't be tempted to rush them by your audience's eyes in a blur.

Indicate what is important. Purposeful movement is effective, and pointing to a key part of a visual will focus the audience's attention. Keep your face turned toward the audience as you point to the screen so that you don't lose eye contact.

Choose simplicity over technological dazzle. Avoid the temptation to impress your audience with special effects. Animations and slide transitions can quickly become annoying or distracting if overused. If you use a laser pointer, restrain yourself from making the red light dance all over the screen.

Avoid reading the visual word for word. This can come across to your audience as condescending. The temptation to read directly off the slide often arises because you've given in to another temptation first: overloading your visual with text. This is one reason to use phrases rather than full sentences. You can supply the extra words and details as you speak.

COMPUTER-GENERATED SLIDE SHOWS

With presentation software—for example, PowerPoint—you can easily develop an impressive slide show. Often, you can arrange to operate a laptop on which you can see the slides, while they are projected on a large screen behind you.

Here are some tips for handling slide shows.

Give yourself a backup plan. You might forget the briefcase that contains your presentation at the airport. Also, technology can be treacherous: You never know when a company server will go down, a projector will fail, a bulb will burn out, or a disk will malfunction.

Effective fail-safe methods include

- bringing hard copies
- emailing yourself a set of slides
- carrying a copy of the presentation on a mini-drive

Try to think of others that will suit your particular situation.

Run through the presentation beforehand. This will boost your confidence in the actual presentation. If you're presenting in an unfamiliar environment, a run-through will also give you a chance to rectify any discrepancies beforehand.

Take care not to block the screen. Find a place to stand so that every member of the audience can see both you and the screen. Often, people won't complain until after the presentation, when it's too late.

Don't race. Some speakers develop a very lengthy presentation and then attempt to race through the slides to finish within the time limit. The audience is bemused and the presentation is a blur—and unlikely to be remembered.

Don't check the screen excessively. Keep your face turned to the audience, and if you must look back at the screen, stop talking. A quick glance now and then should be enough to see that the graphic is properly placed. Provide yourself with notes in large type and a copy of your slides, or position the computer or projector in front of you, so that you can glance at the slide discreetly without losing eye contact with the audience. You may be nervous at the opening, but avoid looking back to check your name and the title of your talk. This move is *not* likely to inspire confidence in your expertise.

Enlist some help. If you can, let someone else operate the computer or projector, so that you will be free to concentrate on the presentation.

TRANSPARENCIES

While computer-generated slides are often a speaker's first choice, some speakers still prefer to use transparencies, even though they do require the use of an overhead projector. They do offer some distinctive ease and flexibility in handling, along with interesting aesthetic possibilities.

A transparency can be fully or partially hand-drawn, either beforehand or on the spot. As you deliver your talk, you can draw and write on a blank plastic sheet. You might work out an equation as you explain a new theory, or draw a line graph in different colors to dramatize the results of an experiment.

If you prepare your transparencies before the talk, you will probably want a more finished effect. The same programs that help with slides can help in designing and producing transparencies, with excellent results.

Transparencies are easy to create, either by printing out hard copies and photocopying onto acetates, or by sending the visuals directly to a printer. Just make sure that you use the right type of acetate sheet for your printer.

Here are some tips in handling transparencies.

Use plastic sleeves. These will facilitate easy handling and help keep your presentation in order.

Place a blank sheet between the sleeves. Now you can read the next transparency easily.

Number your transparencies. These slippery visuals may suddenly slither to the floor and need a quick reordering.

Use caution when printing. There are different types of acetate sheets for laser and dot-matrix printers. If you use a laser printer, use laser-type acetates, or a very expensive meltdown could occur.

Expect the unexpected and prepare for it. Some speakers take along a set of transparencies with their computer-generated slides, just in case of a technology failure. If the slide projector fails, your presentation disk becomes corrupted, or your network crashes, you may be able to hunt down an old overhead projector and save the day.

35MM SLIDES

These have several drawbacks. They can be cumbersome and expensive, they require a darkened room for best visibility, and they need careful arranging in the slide tray to avoid backward or upside-down slides. If you use them, here are some tips.

Create and arrange your slides well in advance. You don't want to discover the upside-down ones in the middle of your talk. Run through your presentation at least once, checking for mistakes.

Avoid talking in the dark. Find a way to provide light for yourself at the lectern so you can read your notes and maintain eye contact with the audience. You also don't want to give anyone an excuse for catching some shuteye.

Coordinate your words and your slides. Wait to project each slide until you are about to discuss it. Give the audience enough time to absorb the information.

Limit the number of slides. Yes, you can fit 100 slides into a carousel, but that doesn't mean you should. Often, just six to 10 slides, carefully selected, may be enough for a 20-minute talk. You may take along extra slides to address possible questions, but you don't have to show them unless the need arises. Presenting too many slides can overwhelm your audience. They may enjoy looking at 30 colorful slides, but they will remember less of your message than if you had used just a few well-chosen slides supported by thorough and interesting commentary.

OPAQUE PROJECTORS

A related technique is the use of opaque projector visuals. The old versions were very noisy and also had the major drawback of requiring a completely darkened room. Newer versions offer the ability to project hard copies, color photos, maps, and 3-D objects, which can be easily projected quietly on a large screen.

PHOTOGRAPHS, PICTURES, AND ILLUSTRATIONS

For detail and accuracy, these visual aids can be used to good effect, provided they are large enough for visibility. Here are some tips.

Wait before you pass them around. If they're too small to be seen from the stage, tell the audience you'll pass them around after the presentation.

Display them only while you are discussing them. Otherwise they become a distraction.

CHALKBOARDS AND WHITEBOARDS

When you're using a chalkboard or whiteboard, try these suggestions.

Use note cards or an outline. Decide in advance what you will put on the board. Your notes or outline will help you remember everything you want to cover. If you plan to use diagrams, draw them in advance. Include labels for all important parts of each drawing.

Hold the chalk properly. Place four fingers on top and your thumb on the bottom, so the chalk doesn't squeak.

Have enough chalk or markers. It's embarrassing to sweep grandly over to the board and then find that the chalk tray contains only dust or the markers are dried out and useless. Have several different colors on hand, too, to emphasize key points.

Plan the physical placement of the writing. Begin writing far enough to the left that there's room for your whole message. Write neatly in lettering large enough to be seen from the back of the room. Check on visibility.

Present your visual support as you talk. You may not want to write anything on the board beforehand unless the writing can be covered up until you're ready to discuss it. Audiences tend to read ahead and may lose concentration on what the speaker is saying.

Practice talking while you write or draw. Glance over your shoulder at your audience while you write. You must talk to your audience and not to the board; otherwise, your listeners may hear only a mumble and attention may flag.

FLIP CHARTS

Easily produced, inexpensive, portable, and reusable, flip charts offer several advantages. You can prepare them ahead of time, or write or draw as you speak—a dramatic touch that can help hold the attention of your listeners.

Flip charts work well for brainstorming meetings. You can list various headings on the chart and then use sticky notes to gather ideas from your audience and organize these ideas under these headings. This idea-generating tool is called an *affinity chart*.

Here are some tips for working with flip charts.

Write clearly and neatly. Wide-tipped felt pens work best for this purpose. But you can pencil in large, neat letters in faint lines first, then go over them with your felt pens.

Keep the lettering very large. Before the presentation, test for good visibility from the last row.

Reveal each page of the flip chart at just the right moment. Wait till you're ready to talk about it or you lose much of its effect. When you've finished with it, remove it.

Avoid distractions. When you're finished with a phase of your presentation, flip the last page over so that the audience isn't drawn back to the chart.

Expect disaster. Anchor your charts firmly, so that they don't tip over during the presentation. If you can't manage a large chart—or any other visual, for that matter—by yourself, recruit someone to help. You don't want to be struggling with an unruly object while speaking.

FILMS AND VIDEOS

When you're handling moving pictures, try these tips.

Keep it short. A long stretch of film can lose the audience's attention. You may want to use only an appropriate segment rather than the whole thing.

Test it first. Make sure the film or video blends in well with your presentation.

See that the room can be darkened enough. Too much light will interfere with clarity.

Check that everyone has a clear view. Sometimes a participant will wait until the end of a presentation to let you know that he or she couldn't see the screen.

HIGH-TECH VISUAL SUPPORT

New computer-based support and Internet access are now available in many presentation rooms. They're valuable tools—if you know how to exploit their potential.

Learn how to use at least one graphics program. Explore the capabilities of the software provided at your company for developing visuals.

Remember: Technology can also get in the way. Use discretion in applying high-tech features. Be sure you're really emphasizing your points and not just distracting your audience.

PHYSICAL OBJECTS

A piece of hardware or a model needs to be large enough for easy viewing by the audience but small enough for easy handling by the speaker. Try these tips.

Select your objects carefully. Resist choosing anything that would be difficult to transport, display, or clean up.

Display the object as you talk about it. Hold it high or walk around with it so that everyone can get a good view.

Avoid fumbling the pass. Hold off until the question-and-answer period to pass around an object. Otherwise you lose the attention of those who are examining the object and those who are waiting for their turn. If you absolutely must pass something around during the talk, take it around yourself, or stop talking until you have regained the audience's attention.

HANDOUTS

When you want to leave something behind with a client, a set of handouts can be a real asset. With well-designed handouts, the audience need take only a few notes. They won't find it as hard to concentrate or be overly engrossed in writing down everything you say. A set of handouts can be a powerful information tool if designed and handled well. Here is some advice.

Provide enough copies. If the group is small enough, provide handouts so that everyone has a set. There is excellent computer software, such as PowerPoint, Freelance Graphics, and Corel Presentations, that will print a reduced-size version of your slides or transparencies, up to six to a page. Providing your audience with handouts will speed their note-taking, but don't supply so much material that they are tempted to stop listening to what you have to say.

Time the distribution of handouts for best effect. The best time to hand material around the group is usually either before you begin or during the question-and-answer period. Avoid handing out anything while you are talking, as this will distract the audience. One exception to this is when you want to take a break from speaking and allow the audience to participate in a hands-on activity or a discussion.

THE KEY GUIDELINES

No matter what kind of visuals you use, here are the most important principles for managing and handling them.

- Choose only visuals that are relevant to your key points.
- Maintain a balance between what you show and what you say.
- Check all visuals for misspellings, wrong usage, and other stylistic flaws.
- Practice! Practice! Practice!

5

Delivering Your Report

You have two options when you walk into a room.
You can own the room. Or it can own you.

—Richard Levick

You have carefully prepared a well-organized talk and you've developed excellent supporting visuals. Now it is time to concentrate on your delivery. Although you have spent a lot of time on what you would say, much of your message depends on nonverbal communication. While the content of your talk is, of course, of primary importance, the way you deliver that content can have a profound effect on the way that your listeners accept your message.

CONTROLLING YOUR BODY

Many speakers, particularly inexperienced ones, are a bit nervous when they first begin to speak. *Telling* yourself to relax may be easy, but actually *doing* it can be quite another matter.

It helps if you can think of your nervousness as a form of energy. Put it to good use and it will give your presentation a dynamic quality. As you prepare yourself by practicing, concentrate on the enthusiasm you feel for your subject. Remind yourself that you really want your listeners to comprehend and appreciate your message.

Here are some ways you can calm anxiety by controlling your physical responses.

Breathing. A good way to calm nerves is to pause and take a deep breath before you begin. A calm, deliberate beginning relieves your nerves and reassures your audience.

Breathe in so deeply that you feel your diaphragm—the muscles around your lower spine—expand. Hold the air for about five to 10 seconds and exhale slowly—then take another deep breath and begin to speak.

Movement. Movement that is graceful and calm, yet energetic, suggests to the audience that you are confident. But holding the body stiffly, or going to the other extreme by fidgeting nervously, can trigger uneasiness or distrust in your listeners.

Aim at moderation. Move for a purpose—for example, to point at the screen. Purposeful movement will not only relieve your own nervousness but also help you hold your audience's attention.

Nervousness can make speakers do strange things—without their even noticing. Therefore, you need to maintain enough awareness of your movement to avoid these awkward practices.

- swaying—this nervous habit tends to hypnotize the audience
- twisting hair or clothing
- clicking your pen or tapping your pencil or pointer
- chewing gum, pen, or finger
- scratching—even if you desperately want to, *don't*

Use of space. Position yourself well in relation to your visual aids, so that you can step back from the podium or your overhead projector to check on your visuals.

Take care to

- avoid blocking the screen with your body
- keep your hand from shadowing your visuals

Gestures. Natural gestures are a great asset to a speaker, while studied or stiff gestures tend to make a speaker look awkward or even ridiculous. Practice in front of a mirror to make sure that your gestures will have the desired effect.

Eye contact. One of the most important aspects of a speaker's facial expression is eye contract. When nervousness attacks, you may feel like burying your nose in the text or focusing intently on your visuals. But listeners tend to equate eye contact with trustworthiness, confidence, and involvement.

Eye contact will help you emphasize points and make your listeners feel that you are interested in them. Looking directly at your listeners is a compelling means of pulling in audience attention. Making direct eye contact with each person in the room helps you convince everyone that you care that your message is getting through to your audience.

Here are five helpful tips concerning eye contact.

- Be so familiar with your material that you can look away from your notes for long periods of time.
- Look at a different person every few seconds or with each new sentence.
- Look around to different parts of the room. Avoid fixing on any one person with a glassy stare. Both of you will become distracted and your listener will feel uncomfortable.
- If you spot someone whose attention seems to have wandered, look intently at that person to draw him or her back.
- Avoid turning around to the screen or chalkboard and talking to your visuals. A glance backward is all you need for a quick check. Look at the visual on the projector instead, so that you can maintain as much eye contact as possible.

CONTROLLING YOUR VOICE

A strong but pleasant voice is a great asset to a speaker. But it's hard to determine the quality of your own voice. Our voices sound different to ourselves than they do to others.

Taping your voice will let you judge its quality accurately. If you don't like what you hear, you can work on improving it. Here are some ways to do just that.

Developing resonance. Many speakers simply do not speak loudly enough. To produce enough volume, you need a confident attitude and a deep breath—and you need to speak *from the diaphragm*.

If you breathe correctly, you will find that you can speak at length without getting hoarse, too. You can test your breathing habits by looking in a mirror and. placing your hands at the sides of your waist. If your hands move out as your waistline expands with a big cushion of air, you are then breathing correctly.

When you take a deep gulp of air, do your shoulders rise? If so, you are breathing incorrectly, and possibly straining your throat muscles to produce your tone.

The action should be taking place in your midsection. Your voice will deepen if you rely on your diaphragm for vocal support.

These two exercises can help you learn to breathe correctly.

Exercise: Breathing

Lie on your back on the floor with a book, cat, baby, or other small object on your stomach. Now breathe so that you raise the small object. Make sure your shoulders do not move. Practice breathing in this way until it feels natural.

Exercise: Projecting

Take a deep breath and hold it at waist level (the location of your diaphragm). Practice projecting your voice with the support of this cushion of air. The effect should be a stronger, more resonant tone.

Lowering pitch. The human ear seems to have an inborn preference for the deeper voice. But many people pitch their voices too high, perhaps through tension or shyness. A man with a squeaky or weak voice commands less authority than the sonorous basso; a woman with a high, whispery voice may be viewed as girlish or timid.

Try to lower your voice as much as you can comfortably manage without sounding unnatural. A low pitch will also allow you to speak longer without fatigue.

Exercise: Pitch

Determine your lowest pitch (which can become lower with practice) by singing down to your lowest note. When you start sounding as if you needed an oil change, stop. Then sing up the scale about four notes. This pitch approximates a comfortable level for your speaking voice.

Strengthen your vocal chords by humming on this pitch, then opening your mouth to "ah-h-h." Be sure the back of your throat is wide open as you do this: imagine that you are about to swallow a whole hard-boiled egg. Start with one minute of vocal exercise and work up to five minutes per day. The beauty of your new tone will amaze you.

Finding the right delivery rate. A rapid-fire delivery rate is difficult to follow. If you race through your talk, your listeners' minds will quickly become numb, particularly if your ideas are fairly complex.

Nor should you speak at a constant rate. Vary your speed. When the material is dense or difficult, speak more slowly; when you have an especially important idea, pause for emphasis.

A good delivery rate averages between 120 and 170 words per minute. You can check your normal rate with the following exercise.

Exercise: Delivery Speed

Select a passage of approximately 500 words (about two double-spaced typed pages). Read it with good expression. If you finish in less than three minutes, you must train yourself to slow down.

Pronouncing your words clearly. As a speaker, you want to sound precise, authoritative, and well educated. But poor language habits can undercut your best efforts to make the right impression.

You may have simply developed bad pronunciation habits, often caused by trying to sound casual. Instead, the effect detracts from the authoritative and knowledgeable impression that you want to make.

Is your articulation clear? Do you avoid mumbling? Do you pronounce words in standard English? The following bad pronunciation habits can detract from your credibility.

Sound substitution

> *d* for *th* (saying *dis* for *this*)
>
> *sh* for *s* (saying *shtop* for *stop*)
>
> *st* for *ss* (saying *acrost* for *across*)

Letter reversal

> *aks* for *ask*

Dropping final sounds, particularly *-in'* for *-ing*

> *closin', goin', doin'*

Exercise: Diction
Listen to yourself on tape. Practice the trouble spots.

Avoiding substandard English. Perfecting one's English is a lifelong task, accomplished by intensive study, reading good books, and listening to good speakers. But until you get a chance to do all this, you can still make an immediate improvement in your English by avoiding barbarisms and clichés like these.

> *like I said*
>
> *have got*
>
> *ain't got*

have went

him and I

me and him

humongous

real bad

mind-boggling

Eliminating verbal static. Some speakers feel compelled to fill in every pause with some kind of sound. The audience, of course, appreciates this as little as it would any other form of static. Too much "um-m-m" and "uh-h-h" and "ah-h-h" and "er-r-r" can spoil the effect of an otherwise excellent presentation.

The same goes for empty, time-filling phrases like these.

at this point in time

due to the fact that

in point of fact

needless to say

in order to

Verbal static keeps your audience from hearing your ideas clearly. But a pause is a wonderful way to hold their interest. If your listeners' minds are wandering, a pause will quickly bring back their attention.

If you cannot remember what you were going to say next, don't panic. Just stop for a second or two. The audience will interpret this moment of silence as a dramatic pause—a chance to reflect on the great wisdom and profundity of what you have just uttered.

Practice avoiding all verbal static in your everyday speech. With a little effort, you can make this habit disappear.

> *Verbal static can reduce a speaker's IQ by 50 points—*
> *at least in the minds of the audience.*

CONTROLLING THE AUDIENCE'S ATTENTION

An experienced speaker has a well-developed awareness of listeners' problems with concentration and comprehension. It is simply much more difficult to take in information by listening rather than by reading.

But if you are aware of these difficulties, you will be better equipped to compensate for the limitations inherent in oral presentation and to benefit from the advantages of a good talk. In short, you can give your listeners what they need and want to hear.

You must consider these barriers to easy comprehension.

The wandering mind. The human mind loves to wander—and uses just about any excuse to do so. Many things can divert listener attention, even if the speaker is interesting. Make a good point and you might still trigger a reverie in the thoughts of your listener, who suddenly drifts away on a tangent. But be a bore and your listener's mind may slip off to the upcoming Friday night bowling, beer, and pizza party.

The linear flow of speech. With a written report, you have the option of backtracking occasionally to review what you have read or clarify some point you've missed. Even if you find yourself daydreaming by the end of the page, you always have the chance to go back. By contrast, speech flows past quickly, and only once. A lapse in attention means that information is lost.

The slow pace of speech. You cannot talk as fast as your listeners can think. The mind can process information at a very rapid rate—which is one reason that a listener so readily loses concentration.

The limits of memory. Research has shown that we humans have a hard time remembering more than *seven items* at a time, unless we have a strong structure in which to place disparate information.

The boundaries of time. When you read a written report, you're free to put it down and read it later. But when you present an oral report, the communication disappears when you finish speaking. If you have only ten minutes to get your ideas across, then you must choose your words very carefully and make sure that the essential message comes through clearly.

The declining attention span. Humans seem to be developing ever shorter attention spans, at least in regard to listening. This may be due to television viewing with its constant commercial interruptions. Researchers have reported that the attention span of a typical college student has shortened to less than seven or eight minutes. Many people can happily spend a whole evening reading, but fewer nowadays seem to have the stamina or the power of concentration to listen for more than a few minutes. That is why you can't just gather a mass of information—no matter how useful—and rattle it off for an hour or two.

Every presentation, no matter how short or how long, needs to be carefully designed to meet all the above challenges.

Here's what you can do to help your listeners.

- Concentrate on maintaining an awareness of audience mood. Do they seem tired? Confused? Bored? Negative?

- Keep lists and categories brief. Limit enumeration to six items or fewer.

- Intensify eye contact and pause—significantly—if you see attention wandering. A sudden silence will bring back the daydreamer's attention immediately.

- Ask if anyone needs a certain point clarified. You may direct questions to your listeners, or ask if they have any questions.

- Backtrack. Repeat key ideas and supply brief internal summaries. Emphasize major points. Oral presentations require more repetition than written material.

- Break up the audience into small "buzz groups" of three to four. Provide the groups with some points to discuss or a problem to solve.

FINAL COURTESIES

Stay within time limits. One of the biggest faults a speaker can have is long-windedness. By its very nature, an oral presentation does not lend itself to exhaustive treatment. An overly dense and detailed presentation will prevent you from getting your ideas across to your listeners vividly and effectively. If you wanted to present your audience with every detail, you would have handed them a written report with numerous appendices.

The speaker most likely to be regarded with fear and loathing is the one who exceeds the allotted time—even by a few minutes.

Keep your conclusion strong. The human mind can absorb information for only as long as the other end can bear to sit. Avoid rambling on; you will only bore your audience. Length is a poor substitute for depth.

A strong, clear, brief conclusion is crucial to the success of your report. This is not the time to run out of steam, nor to run off at the mouth. Use your conclusion to reemphasize the core of your message.

Give your listeners a signpost, such as "In conclusion, I want to emphasize that …" or "As a final point, I wish to say …." (Refer back to Ch. 2 for some suggestions for good conclusions.) Then make certain that you deliver your very last sentence—which is a strong statement, of course—with emphasis and great confidence.

Make the question-and-answer period work. Sometimes this turns into one of the best parts of the presentation. With some preparation, you can ensure that it is worthwhile.

First, set up some ground rules. When you're preparing your talk, decide when you want to field questions. Here are some useful strategies.

- Allow interruptions for questions at any time
- Stop for several question breaks during the talk before moving from one major point to the next
- Take questions only at the end

If your presentation has a time limit, you will probably want to wait until after the conclusion. You don't want to risk using up your time on a long-winded questioner halfway through your report.

Try to anticipate questions that might come up. Prepare some appropriate answers in advance.

When you're ready to take questions, leave the slide that states your conclusions up on the screen. This will help the audience focus their thoughts.

Announce the question-and-answer period with a simple statement: "Does anyone have any questions?" or "I will now respond to any questions you may have." Set a limit for this period, to reduce the chance that someone will try to engage you in a tiresome debate. If this happens, politely ask the debater to wait for further discussion until after the session is finished.

What if no one has a question? Don't stand there in embarrassment as an uncomfortable silence settles over the room. Try to have a few questions prepared in advance that *you* can ask *your audience*. Then, if you have time left over, you can ask if anyone would like to discuss one of them. One such question is usually enough to loosen up your audience.

Otherwise, simply smile warmly, thank your listeners, and sit down. In short, follow this time-honored advice for making a graceful exit:

Be sincere, be brief . . . be seated!

6

Twenty Surefire Tips...

*Those who can make you believe absurdities
can make you commit atrocities.*

—Voltaire

Did you know there would be a quiz? The time has arrived to test your knowledge of presentation skills and techniques.

Place a check in front of each suggestion that you consider a *good idea*.

☐ *Put it off a little longer.* If you cannot resist preparing, at least wait until the night before to begin. This will give you a fine high-strung energy for your talk, and your bloodshot eyes will generate sympathy.

☐ *Don't outline.* True spontaneity is a noble ideal. You may even surprise yourself with what you say during the presentation.

☐ *Don't practice.* Being too smooth makes your audience insecure. A bit of stumbling on your part will make them feel vastly superior—always a good ploy.

☐ *Dress down.* Don't give the impression that you think what you have to say is important.

☐ *Look modestly at the floor.* Don't make eye contact—it makes you look too confident, as though you think you know what you're talking about.

☐ *Be very, very subtle.* Hint indirectly at the purpose of your talk—or better yet, don't mention it at all. Your listeners will think your material is deeper if they have trouble figuring it out.

☐ *Mumble.* Just to be safe, keep them unsure of exactly what you're saying.

☐ *Pad with verbal static.* Generous use of "uh" and "y'know" and "OK" will give your presentation a charmingly unstudied air. Enough deadwood can stretch a five-minute talk into a full 10 minutes. Much more impressive!

☐ *Toss in some substandard English.* Cultivate a "good ol' boy" effect. Some double negatives and ungrammatical phrases will keep you from sounding like a snob.

☐ *Use long words.* Replace short, clear words with as many ponderous polysyllabic ones as possible. You'll impress your listeners with your erudition.

☐ *Fidget.* Fiddle with a sleeve button or a paper clip or your hair. Sway or shuffle your feet. You don't want them to think you're too cool and collected.

☐ *Use every visual you can think of.* Bombard your audience with at least 50 to 100 slides. The more images you present, one right after another, the greater effect each one will have.

☐ *Make it flashy.* Take full advantage of all the wonderful animated effects and brilliant colors available to make your computer-generated slide show really dazzling. Otherwise your audience will have nothing to hold their attention but your ideas.

☐ *Don't waste time testing your slides.* If they look good on your computer screen, they will look even better when projected.

☐ *Don't put your transparencies in holders.* The interesting effect that results when they stick together is well worth the effort. You may even be able to show four or five of them at once.

☐ *Don't number your transparencies.* When you drop them, they will fall out of order, giving you an excellent opportunity to improvise for the rest of your talk.

☐ *Display your most complicated equations.* Dazzle your audience with your mathematical abilities. Make them use their brains. Why should you do all the intellectual work?

☐ *Don't leave anything out.* Stuff every bit of information you have into your presentation. Trust your colleagues and clients to figure out for themselves what you think is important and what's not.

☐ *Never use humor.* Professionals are supposed to be serious. An occasional lame or overused joke is acceptable, but being genuinely witty undercuts your authority.

☐ *Monopolize.* When you speak on a panel or at a conference, take up as much of the available time as you can. Your rambling is more spellbinding than anything the others may have to say. If you use up all the time, it's just the next speaker's tough luck.

Give yourself 5 points for every right answer.   Score_____

What? You didn't check off *anything*? Good for you! Give yourself a perfect 100, because the name of this chapter really ought to be

Twenty Surefire Tips...
for a Truly Disastrous Presentation!

Every one of these tips is at best misguided and at worst blatantly false. Using even a few of them could ensure that you're never asked to speak again.

If, on the other hand, you think you can handle all the success that comes from being a skillful speaker, here is my recommendation:

Violate all these suggestions, every last one—
every time you take the stage—and then get ready
to enjoy the great appreciation and enthusiastic applause
that a really fine speaker deserves.

Appendices

A Presentation Planner 72

B Worksheet: Choosing Your Title 76

C Using Mnemonics 78

D Transitions 79

E Speaker Self-Evaluation Worksheet 81

APPENDIX A
PRESENTATION PLANNER

Focusing Your Ideas

What is your *general* purpose in giving this presentation? Some talks have more than one purpose, so check all that apply.

☐ to inform   ☐ to warn   ☐ to inspire

☐ to instruct   ☐ to persuade   ☐ to honor

☐ to actuate   ☐ to recommend   ☐ to thank

What is your *specific* purpose? Complete this sentence: After this talk, my audience will _____

_____

_____

What is the central idea underlying your presentation? State this as a complete sentence.

_____

_____

Are there any special audience considerations you need to work with? Think about audience attitudes, beliefs, and values in relation to your topic.

_____

_____

Choose an interesting and appropriate title for your presentation. Use App. B if you need some guidance.

_____

_____

Introduction

Remember that your opening segment must accomplish these tasks: introducing your topic, getting the audience's favorable attention and motivating them to listen, giving them a preview of what you'll say, and establishing your credibility as a speaker.

Attention-grabbing opening

_____

_____

Statement of purpose

_____

_____

Preview of key points

_____

_____

Body

Your first key point

_____

_____

Your support for this point

_____

_____

Your transition to the next point (see App. D for guidance)

_____

_____

Your second key point

_____

_____

Your support for this point

_____

_____

Your transition to the next point

_____

_____

Your third key point

_____

_____

Your support for this point

_____

_____

Your transition to the conclusion

_____

_____

Conclusion

Focus again on your main purpose and briefly review your key points.

_____

_____

What will you use as a memorable closer?

☐ striking example   ☐ request for buy-in   ☐ clear question

☐ compelling statistic   ☐ illustrative analogy   ☐ vision of the future

☐ pertinent anecdote ☐ vivid graphic ☐ other: _____

☐ call for action ☐ pertinent quotation

Take care that your closer relates directly to your presentation. Avoid introducing any new points.

Question-and-Answer Period

Think of some questions your audience might ask. Then prepare answers for them.

Possible questions

1. _____

_____

2. _____

_____

3. _____

_____

Your answers

1. _____

_____

2. _____

_____

3. _____

_____

APPENDIX B
WORKSHEET: CHOOSING YOUR TITLE

A good title can engage your audience's interest in what's to come. Here are some types of titles you can consider.

Simple Statement of Topic

This kind of title can be effective, but sometimes it needs something more to get the audience's interest.

- Assertiveness Techniques for Women at Work
- Integrating Fiberoptic Networks
- How to Secure a Small Business Loan

Ideas for your presentation

_____

_____

_____

Question Title

Question titles tend to sound informal, so they best fit an informal speaking situation.

- Is Upper Management out of Touch?
- How Can ABC Company Reduce Manufacturing Costs?
- What Was the Impact of Upgrading the Manufacturing Line?

Ideas for your presentation

_____

_____

_____

Creative Title

This kind of title usually combines a straightforward descriptive phrase with a question or an imaginative, dramatic, or metaphoric phrase.

- Tilting to the Left and Right: Broadcasting and the Public Interest
- Broadband: Is it Right for Our Company?
- The Good, the Bad, and the Ugly: A Status Report on Laboratory Equipment

Ideas for your presentation

_____

_____

_____

Now pick the one that you like the best.

APPENDIX C
USING MNEMONICS

Here are some devices that can help your listeners remember your ideas.

Acronyms

> KISS: Keep It Simple, Sailor
>
> MYOB: Managing Your Optics Business
>
> RICE: Rest, Ice, Compression, Elevation

Alliteration

> Manufacturing, Manpower, Money
>
> The Big Question: Quantity vs. Quality
>
> Style, Service, Selection, Satisfaction

Repetition

> Better employee performance
>
> Better customer satisfaction
>
> Better bottom line

Generics

> The ABCs of…
>
> The Seven Habits of Highly Effective…
>
> The Ten Commandments of…
>
> The Three Rs of…

APPENDIX D
TRANSITIONS

In any presentation, you're traveling down an information highway with your audience, and you need to guide them visually and verbally so they'll end up where you want them. By using well-chosen transitional words and phrases to lead them from one idea to the next, you can provide coherence and clarity.

Transitions need to be even stronger in an oral presentation than they do in a written report. A reader who doesn't understand something can stop and reread, or even turn back and review an earlier section; a listener can't. Even a momentary misunderstanding may cause an audience member to misinterpret your most important points.

In giving your presentation, then, you need to provide the audience with some useful signposts.

Transitions indicate the direction of your thoughts, the relationships from idea to another or from section to the next. They signal the importance of key information, and help your audience stay focused on it.

There are many kinds of transitions.

Maps. Use preparatory transitions to map out the direction your talk will take.

> *There are three significant advantages to this. First...*

> *Let me explain how we developed this policy...*

> *There are two basic approaches we could take. I want to compare their plusses and minuses...*

Billboards. Use emphasis transitions to alert your audience that a really important point is coming up.

> *Our testing revealed that one factor affects these results far more than any other...*

> *Surprisingly, four out of five of our customers responded with the same answer...*

> *But a new technology we're developing will change all this...*

Turn signals. Use directive transitions to indicate a change of direction in your talk.

> *Now let's look more carefully at three good ways we can increase production. First...*

> *However, this rule of thumb has an important exception...*

> *That sums up the advantages of this method. Now let's look at the disadvantages...*

Road markers. You can use milestone transitions to mark the various phases of your presentation.

> *Now that I've defined the problem, let's look at some possible solutions...*

> *That's the history of the division in a nutshell. What about plans for the immediate future?*

> *I want to turn away from theory now and look at some practical considerations...*

APPENDIX E
SPEAKER SELF-EVALUATION WORKSHEET

Step 1

Videotape yourself giving your presentation.

Step 2

Watch your performance and evaluate it with the help of the following worksheet.

Title

What is the title of your talk? _____

Is your title interesting? _____

Visuals

What is the length of your talk in minutes? _____

How many visuals do you have? _____

Do you use about one visual per minute? _____

Speaking Ability

Comment on each of the following aspects of your performance.

     appearance   _____

     poise   _____

     eye contact   _____

     pace of speech   _____

     pronunciation   _____

     volume of voice   _____

     tone of voice   _____

     gestures   _____

     avoiding verbal static   _____

What can be improved? _____

_____

Introduction

Rate your introduction for each of the following aspects.

stating central idea clearly	Excellent Good Fair Poor
gaining audience's favorable attention	Excellent Good Fair Poor
motivating audience to listen	Excellent Good Fair Poor
previewing main points	Excellent Good Fair Poor
establishing your credibility	Excellent Good Fair Poor

What can be improved? _____

_____

Body

Rate the body of your presentation for each of the following aspects.

providing appropriate background	Excellent Good Fair Poor
defining terms	Excellent Good Fair Poor
giving interesting examples	Excellent Good Fair Poor
interesting and effective visual support	Excellent Good Fair Poor
making clear and effective transitions	Excellent Good Fair Poor
giving helpful signposts along the way	Excellent Good Fair Poor

What can be improved? _____

_____

Conclusion

Rate the conclusion of your presentation for each of the following aspects.

summarizing main points	Excellent Good Fair Poor
restating thesis in an interesting way	Excellent Good Fair Poor
closing effectively and memorably	Excellent Good Fair Poor

What can be improved? _____

_____

Overall

Rate your presentation overall for each of the following aspects.

topic appropriate for audience	Excellent Good Fair Poor
level and quality of information	Excellent Good Fair Poor
presentation above the ordinary	Excellent Good Fair Poor

What can be improved? _____

_____

Final Questions

What was the best aspect of your talk?

_____

What needs the most improvement?

_____

Further Reading

Designing Presentations

Alley, Michael. *The Craft of Scientific Presentations: Critical Steps to Succeed and Critical Errors to Avoid.* Springer. Many interesting examples of scientists as presenters help explain what makes a presentation work. Offers some refreshing new views on how to design a speech and support it visually, including some improved ways to incorporate graphics and text into computer-based projections. A very useful section on the design of scientific posters.

Atkinson, Cliff. *Beyond Bullet Points: Using PowerPoint to Create Presentations That Inform, Motivate, and Inspire.* Microsoft Press. Argues that slides should be triggers for what the speaker wants to say. Sees a talk as a dramatic performance that works best as a balanced blend of message and media. Offers useful and sophisticated methods for focusing ideas, developing a storyboard, integrating text and graphics, using the notes pages feature, and heightening audience appeal.

Craig, Malcolm. *Thinking Visually: Business Applications of 14 Core Diagrams.* Continuum International. Shows and explains 14 diagrams that can function as core building blocks of diagramming. Actual cases from industry and business demonstrate practical use.

Harris, Robert L. *Information Graphics: A Comprehensive Illustrated Reference.* Oxford University Press. Covers all kinds of visual support with information arranged alphabetically for easy access.

Tufte, Edward. *Envisioning Information.* Graphics Press. Award-winning book for content and design, with many new insights on displaying data graphically.

Tufte, Edward R. *The Cognitive Style of PowerPoint.* Graphics Press. Critical of the overuse of "slideware" at the expense of genuine analysis. Encourages speakers to base their presentations on original verbal and spatial reasoning and real statistical analysis in place of ready-made templates and designs.

Wempen, Faithe. *PowerPoint Advanced Presentation Techniques.* John Wiley & Sons. Good tips on how to avoid the monotony of bullet list presentations. In-depth explanations of how to work with graphics and templates of all kinds.

Developing Speaking Technique

Axtell, Roger E. *Do's and Taboos of Public Speaking: How to Get Those Butterflies Flying in Formation.* John Wiley & Sons. Valuable tips on managing stage fright. Excellent information on special speaking situations such as appearing on television. The author has also written guides for those who must work in international trade or speak to foreign audiences.

Beebe, Steven A., and John T. Masterson. *Communicating in Small Groups: Principles and Practices.* Allyn & Bacon. Covers a wide range of topics in group communication and dynamics, leadership, and team building.

Jacobi, Jeffrey. *How to Say It with Your Voice.* Prentice Hall Press. A Fortune 500 voice coach provides a method for achieving a dynamic and confident speaking style through developing the voice for power and authority. Recommends ways to eliminate unwanted vocal qualities (monotone, breathiness, and so on), eliminate vocalized pauses, tone down regional accents, and cure sloppy pronunciation. (Interactive CD included.)

Nice, Shirley E. *Speaking for Impact: Connecting With Every Audience.* Allyn & Bacon. Provides useful materials on audience analysis (concrete versus abstract thinkers) and emphasizes credibility, levels of impact, connection, and passion for one's subject.

O'Connor, J. Regis. *High-Impact Public Speaking for Business and the Professions.* McGraw Hill. The author sees public speaking as one of the great power tools for driving business. Includes model speeches by business leaders such as Lee Iacocca.

Ready, Anne Cooper. *Off the Cuff: What to Say at a Moment's Notice.* Barnes & Noble Books. Focuses on situations requiring impromptu speaking: networking, interviewing, phone calls, conferencing, trade shows, panels, workshops, seminars, and meetings.

PROFESSIONAL PUBLICATIONS, INC.

Index

35 mm slide, 49
Aesthetic appeal, 42, 46
Affinity chart, 51
Animation, 41
Arrow callout, 36–37
Attention
    audience, 62–63
    focusing, 22, 62–63
Audience
    analysis, 5, 17
    focusing attention, 22, 62–63
    informational need, 17
    involving, 15
Background, slide, 42
Body of talk, 16
Breathing, 56, 58
Buzz group, 63
Central idea, 3
Chalkboard, 51
Chart slide, 28
Clarity, 40–41
Closing technique, 18–19, 35
Color combination, 42–43, 46
Conclusion, 18, 64, 74–75
Consistency, 41–42
Controlling
    material, 4
    voice, 58–61

Critique, visual, 43, 46
Delivery, 55–65
    mode, 8
    rate, 59–60
Diagram slide, 29
Diction, 60–61
Disastrous presentation, how to create,
    67–69
Discussion (body of talk), 16
Ending, memorable, 18
Equipment, 6–7
    projection, 23
Extemporaneous talk, 8, 11
Eye contact, 57
Fail-safe method, 7, 47–48
Failure, system, 7
Feedback, 46
Film, 52
Flip chart, 51–52
Focusing attention, 22
Font size, 40
Gesture, 57
Handling visuals, 45–47
Handout, 7, 39, 53–54
High-tech visuals, 53
HUG and KISS, 44
Illustration, 50
Impromptu talk, 8

Informational need, 17
Introduction to talk, 14–15, 73
Introductory visuals, 31
Key points, 3–4, 18, 22, 36, 73
    slide, 36
Keyhole pattern, 13–14
KISS and HUG, 44
Label, 37
Lectern, 10
Limit
    memory, 62
    time, 63
Major points, 3–4, 18, 22, 36, 73
Manuscript talk, 9–10
Mathematical
    slide, 25, 30
    transparency, 49
Memorized speech, 8–9
Memory, 78
    aiding, 19, 22, 42
    appeal, 42
    limit, 62
Method of presentation, 8
Mind, wandering, 62
Mnemonics, 78
Mode of delivery, 8
Movement, 56
Need, informational, 17
Nervousness, 56
Note card, 11
Notes pages, 39
Notes, speaker's, 11
Objective, 2
Object as visual aid, 53
Opaque projector, 50
Organization, 16–17
Outlining, 4, 11
Overview slide, 31–32, 33
Photograph, 50
    as slide, 27, 32
Physical setting, 6
Pictorial slide, 26–27
Picture, 50
Pitch, lowering, 59
Planner, presentation, 72
Planning, visuals, 23
Poster, 38
PowerPoint, 39

Practice, 45–47
Presentation
    method, 8
    planner, 72
    software, 39, 41
    structure, 13
Projection
    equipment, 23
    screen, 48
    vocal, 58
Projector, opaque, 50
Pronunciation, 60
Purpose, clarifying, 2, 72
Question-and-answer period, 14, 20, 38, 39, 64–65, 75
Rate of delivery, 59–60
Resonance, 58
Screen, projection, 48
Self-evaluation, 81
Setting, physical, 6
Simplicity, 41
Slide
    35 mm, 49–50
    background, 42
    chart, 28
    diagram, 29
    key point, 36
    overview, 31–32, 33
    photograph, 27, 32
    pictorial, 26–27
    poor design, 31–34
    show, computer-generated, 24, 47
    summary, 38
    title, 31–32
    verbal, 25–26
Software, presentation, 39, 41
Space, use of, 56–57
Speaker's notes, 11
Statement of purpose, 2
Static, verbal, 61
Storyboard, 24
Structure, presentation, 13
Summary, 18
    slide, 38
    visual, 19
System failure, preparing for, 7
Time limit, 63

Title, 76
   slide, 31–32
Transition, 18, 73–74, 79
Transparency, 40, 48–49
   mathematical, 49
Variety, 42
Verbal
   slide, 25–26
   static, 61
Video, 52
Visibility, 40, 50–51, 52
Visual villains, 43
Visuals, 17, 21–44
   critique, 43, 46
   determining content, 24
   handling, 45–47
   introductory, 31
   persuasive qualities, 22
   planning, 23
   projection equipment, 23
   summary, 19
   variety, 22
Voice
   control, 58–61
   lowering pitch, 59
Wandering mind, 62
Whiteboard, 51